96
p98, 106, 109, 111, 114, 122, 130, 136, 143

Winston Jones

THE WAY IT WAS
IN A
RURAL COMMUNITY

by

WINSTON JONES

Published by
Rhosygwalia Books

Published in 2010 by
Rhosygwalia Books
Triolbrith, Rhos, Llangeler
Llandysul, Carms., SA44 5AE

The right of Winston Jones to be identified as the Author of the Work has been asserted by him in accordance with the Copyright, Designs and Patents Act 1988.

A CIP catalogue record for this book is available from the British Library

ISBN 978-0-9553343-1-3

Printed and bound in Wales by
Gomer Press Ltd.
Llandysul Enterprise Park, Llandysul
Ceredigion, SA44 4JL

Dedicated to my two sisters Mair and Priscilla, and my brother Gwynoro, remembering the happy times we had when we were growing up, and remembering the love and support that were unfailingly given when times were hard. Also my children – Helen, Colin, and Mark, and my grand daughter, Stephanie, who have always been there for me.

ACKNOWLEDGEMENTS

First of all I would like to thank my wife Gill for typing this script, for correcting any grammatical or spelling errors, for scanning the photographs, and putting the whole on disc. Without her, this book would not have seen the light of day.

I would also like to thank the following for giving their permission to reproduce photographs:

The University of Reading

Llyfrgell Genedlaethol Cymru/The National Library of Wales

Clwb Hanes Llanfihangel-ar-Arth Local History Club

Getty Images, London

Ken Jones, Bryn Haul, Newcastle Emlyn

The Thomson family, Henllan, Llandysul

I would also like to extend my heartfelt thanks to Gomer Press, Llandysul for printing this book.

CONTENTS

INTRODUCTION

I publish this book with all due modesty, for I am not a historian, but only a compiler of stories that I remember from my younger days. Also, I have drawn on my own experiences of a lifetime of farm work and rural community life, and have commented on the social changes that have occurred over the last hundred years. I make reference as well to the Stone and Bronze Ages and the Roman occupation, to put what I'm saying in context. Where I have used references (see bibliography), I have used them - not as a research tool - but merely to confirm what I already knew from my own experience.

I was fortunate enough to have spent a lot of time with people who had grown up at the turn of the last century but one. When they started pouring out their memories upon my generation, they knew only too well that with their passing, all personal knowledge of that age would disappear for ever.

Yr hen ŵr llwyd o'r cornel   *The grey old man of the corner*

Gan ei dad a glywodd chwedl   *Of his father heard a story*

A chan ei dad fe glywodd yntau *Which from his father he had heard*

Ac ar ei ôl mi gofiais innau   *And after them I have remembered*

(D. Parry Jones, 1953, p.13)

I hope that I will open a door for the younger generation, and also for the many newcomers to the district, some of whom have come from city life and have settled in the countryside, because I know that many of these people are eager to learn about the way of life in this part of the country, and learn the local folk lore. There is now a generation growing up here who, if we are not careful, will know very little about their birthplace, or the lanes, woods and fields through which they roam. One of the reasons for this could be that children nowadays are taken to and from school by car. Children now miss out on chatting to different people and stopping by gateways to see things from a different angle - as I did. It seems to me to be a shame that children might be deprived of the opportunity to absorb things about their own locality.

Over the years, perhaps since the Second World War, the countryside has changed dramatically, and people have had to change accordingly. The motor car has given us the ability to go from one place to another very quickly and comfortably, but by so doing, has robbed us of time on the road - to meet other people, to spend more time with them, and to slow each other down to that pace which we all seem to have forgotten.

A perfect example of the leisurely pace of life

(Museum of English Rural Life – MERL - University of Reading)

The system which had been developed on the farms over the previous 200 years relied on a partnership between horse-power and hand-power. Also, there was a common bond between the farmer and the cottager – the farmer depending on the cottager for labour, and the cottager depending on the farmer for work, and for the loan of a machine, or perhaps a horse and gambo - if a member of his family was moving, or if he wanted to fetch something from the local railway station. Wages were low, but there was a strict rule that people looked out for each other. No-one went without – there was plenty of free milk, logs, potatoes, and rabbits.

The end of a working day

(The Eric Guy Collection, MERL, University of Reading)

Then came the tractor. For a time, it was quite common to see a tractor and a couple of horses working on the same farm. But gradually the tractor took over, and the horse almost disappeared. This is the reason that there are far less workers on the land now than there have ever been. With the coming of the tractor, the fields at harvest time lost a quality which they had possessed - the quality which gave one the sense of turning the pages of a history book. By this I mean that when the workers started on one field – perhaps turning the hay, or stacking corn, or working in the potato field – they would start to reminisce. The stories that would be told in one field were the same every year – perhaps it would be the story of the fasting girl, or the murder in Blaenduad, or the fisherman's tale. There would be a different story told in each field, and as the work finished on a particular field for that year, the story would also end. When work started on the next field, another story would be retold - it was as if they were turning the pages of a history book. I hope to bring back to mind some of these ways of life that I remember - and also some that I don't remember because it was before my day, and relayed to me by my elders.

Perhaps I should mention here that the chapters I most enjoyed writing were from chapter nine on. This is because I was writing about the time when I lived and grew up: I was a part of it, and because of that, I remember the changes so clearly. To me, then was the present time. The earlier chapters I have included merely to set the scene – they are historical facts passed down from generation to generation.

I recognise that changes have always taken place – not only in rural communities, but also in other industries such as in the woollen, coal, and slate industries - in fact in all spheres including the medical and teaching professions. But I have written about what I know, from being a part of it. I have also tried to abide by any copyright rules. If I have broken any, forgive me.

CHAPTER 1
My Native Parish

During the sixth century a Christian pilgrim and missionary by the name of Celer arrived in these parts and founded the parish church. It was thus called St Geler by the people, and still is to this day. Thus Llangeler was born (Llan meaning church – Llangeler, the church of Celer).

The parish of Llangeler lies in the northwest of Carmarthenshire, with the river Teifi forming the boundary to the North. On the other side of the Teifi lies the county of Cardigan, or Ceredigion. Separating the parish from that of Llanfihangel-ar-Arth (on the east side from Pontweli) the boundary for a few hundred yards is the river Tweli, until the river Gwyddil joins it. The boundary now follows the river Gwyddil all the way to its source, not far from Carreghir. To the south, the boundary separating the parish of Llangeler from that of Cynwyl Elfed is an almost straight line running from Carreghir through the middle of Cruglas reaching the river Bargoed, which separates the parish of Llangeler from that of Penboyr.

Standing in our parish at a particular spot near Carreghir, it is possible to shake hands with a person standing in the parish of Llanfihangel-ar-Arth, and also to shake hands with another person standing in the parish of Cynwyl Elfed, for it is at this spot that the three parishes meet (and before the boundaries of the parishes were changed, the parish of Llanpumsaint was a fourth).

The highest point in the parish is in the south. This moorland is called Rhos Llangeler, and consisted of open common land until the Enclosures Act of 1866, when it began to become claimed. Until that time only a very small part of it had been claimed by squatters, each building their one night house – the 'Ty Unnos' – and claiming a few acres around the house. Most of these one-night houses lay between the road coming up from Pentrecwrt to Penlôn, near Clais, and the main road leading to Carmarthen, where St James' Church now stands. The rest of the Rhos was open moorland as far as Tyhen and Glaspant, following the road that goes past Penclawdd towards Penboyr. This imaginary line forms a natural boundary – the lower land in the parish being split into holdings and farmed earlier (see below), whereas the higher land is mostly peat, and quite stony. When ploughing the upper land, large stones are encountered – sometimes six feet across and more. Some of these are grey granite, and some are quartz – the white stone. I remember my father saying on several occasions that if the land had to be stony, it was better to have grey stone than white because the grey stone is always warm, whereas the white is always cold, even on a hot summer's day. I know this to be true from my own experience. The rest of the parish, below my imaginary line, became enclosed (separated into holdings) and farmed from about the sixteen and seventeen hundreds on.

Some holdings had streams as boundaries, others roads or lanes, and others hedges. Members of the family had to take it in turns to shepherd the cattle to keep the animals off the crops and so on. A Parliamentary Act was passed in 1783 that farmers should construct so many chains of hedge per annum. This resulted in most of the fields being hedged in. Ordinance surveyors would then come and measure each field, giving each an OS number. Every farmer didn't comply too well with the new regulations – probably because they didn't want to change from the old ways of shepherding the cattle. So, in 1803, another Act of Parliament was passed, forcing every farmer to comply. I have observed that small farms have small fields, and that bigger farms have bigger fields.

At the time of the first Act of 1783, the Napoleonic Wars were raging, and there was a real risk that this country would be subject to a French invasion. To defend a country with numerous hedges was far easier than to defend open countryside. Of course, we all know that there were fields and hedges to be had in some parts of Britain long before this time, but the practice was not widespread. It is worth remembering, when we look at the fields and hedges of today, that they were constructed to keep out enemies, or at least to try and keep them out. This practice of using hedges and walls for defence purposes has been in existence for many hundreds of years. Hadrian's Wall, for example, between the rivers Tyne and Salway was meant to keep out the enemy from the North. Much nearer home, the *'clawdd mawr'* – between Cwmduad and Penboyr – had a similar purpose. The latter is thought to have been there since the Stone Age.

I cannot imagine a country without fields and hedges where livestock can shelter and be kept safe from wandering, not to mention valuable habitats for wildlife. We are all indebted to the people who gave us the hedges over two hundred years ago.

The most fertile half of the parish is in the lower part, towards the river Teifi, with its lush meadowland and rich soil. The landscape of the parish on the whole, in my opinion, has a beauty that can be compared favourably with the landscape in any other part of Wales. There are beautiful rivers and streams which have – over hundreds of thousands of years – cut deep ravines into the terrain. As these rivers and streams make their way down from the uplands, some people describe them as small, swift, and talkative. They run for anything from about two miles to about five before joining a bigger stream or river. They are not always visible as they lie hidden in deep wooded glens, but they can always be heard as they skip over the stones and rush around bends, serving a very useful purpose as boundaries between farms. I feel I must mention the beauty of the river Teifi at Henllan bridge – including in fact all along the Teifi past Alltcafan bridge, which T. Llew Jones described so well in his song 'Bont Alltcafan'.

The parish was split up - probably around 1146, when the Cistercian Monastery was built in Whitland by the Norman Bishop

Bernard (the monastery is now known as Whitland Abbey). Bishop Bernard gave half of the parish to the monastery at Whitland, and this part was known as the Grange - 'Y Gransh'. The other half was known as 'Y Wlad'. The Grange remained under the ownership of Whitland Abbey until it finally became Crown land at the Dissolution of the Monasteries in 1536. It remained under Crown ownership for the next hundred years until the reign of Charles 1st, when part of it was bought by John Lewes of Llysnewydd.

The two parts of the parish were called the Emlyn Manor to the West and the Maenor Forian Grange to the East. The boundary between these was the lane going from the moor past Triolmaengwyn, Penlôn, then became the lane passing Rhydybennau. Then from Glanrhyd bridge ('bont Glanrhyd'), it follows the river Shedi until it reaches the Teifi river.

From the beginning of the eighteen hundreds, most of the parish of Llangeler was under the ownership of the Lewes's, of the Llysnewydd Estate. Mr Lewes was known as the Lord of the Manor Forian Grange. The Llysnewydd Estate at that time extended from Rhos, Llangeler, and included Bancyffordd,

Llangeler, Henllan, and a large part of Cardiganshire – namely Llanaeron and Llanllyr. But today most of the estate has been sold.

The Leet Court (*'Y Cwrt Clyd'*)

The court was held to deal with any tenant, or anyone else for that matter, who abused the rules regarding the common land. The following account is taken from Daniel E. Jones' (1899, p.71) excellent book *'Hanes Plwyfi Llangeler a Phenboyr'* (translated from the Welsh, by the author).

The Lord of the Manor of Llysnewydd was responsible for ensuring that there was a warden, which in these days would be called a ranger, to look after the common land of the Grange. Local farmers and smallholders were the tenants of the common. The title of the Lord of the Manor was somewhat precarious, as the Lord of the Manor had to pay £14.16s. to the Crown annually for the title, and this was quite a financial burden for him. He was, in fact, no more than a tax collector for the Crown, because all the rent he collected had to be passed on to the Crown, and was called the Crown Rent. If any one of the tenants broke the rules, he would be summoned to appear in the Leet Court. In our area, most people think the court was held in the farm called Cwrt (meaning court), but according to Daniel E. Jones (1899 p.71), the court was actually held in Coylanfelen, a nearby farm (incidentally, I think that the court probably existed before the village of Pentrecwrt ('*pentref*', village, '*cwrt*', court) because it derives its name from the court). This is what one of the notices said:

> *The Court Leet will be held at Coylanfelen on the 19th of October the first year of the reign of our Lord King William the Fourth, and in the year of our Lord, 1830, when Thomas Davies, Coylanfelen, will be steward of the court, and the following will be Jurymen of this court, Evan Evans, Penpistyll, David Williams, Llwynffynon Uchaf, Evan Thomas, Brafle, Evan Jones, Shadog, David Jones, Cwrt, Daniel James, Blaenshedi, John Thomas, Glyncoch, Jams Williams, Blaenantrhys, David Jones, Glanshedi, David Jones, Felin Cwrt, and Thomas Evans, Gaerwenuchaf.*

Anyone who didn't attend the court after being summoned was fine 2s.6d. The court dealt mostly with animals straying off the common, and it was the responsibility of the Lord of the Manor to employ a keeper and a constable of the pound or fold to hold any straying cattle. Another rule was that no-one was allowed to sell any peat to anyone living outside the boundaries of the Grange. New tenants had to pay 10s.6d deposit to the Lord of the Manor.

Some of the fines were as follows:

- For damaging a hedge – 1s to 10s
- Sending animals to graze without permission – 10s 6d
- Letting animals stray on the road – 6d
- Letting animals stray at night – 10s
- Turning out horses one day too soon – 2s
- Not gathering stones on the common – 1s

Everyone who sent animals on to the common had to pay 3s.4d towards the wages of the chief steward. They would also be fined if they sent their cattle or sheep on to the common before the steward or ranger had sounded his horn.

The pound for the Grange was near Bwlchmelyn. The last keeper of the pound was a William Jones.

There was always a very good turnout every time the court was held. It was something of a general holiday, where people would eat and drink. It was regarded as some sort of festival – probably a relic of a practice of some bygone age, when the prince himself would come and spend nine nights in the locality - he would stay with different people, all of whom would give their food and wine freely.

CHAPTER 2
Rhos, Llangeler

The village of Rhos as it is today has only been in existence for the last thirty or forty years at the most. There used not to be a village there at all. Travelling down the main road before about 1870, from where St James' Church now stands, there were only two houses – Pencae and Maespant. Turning right at Maespant, there was only one house – Pantbach, before coming to Penwaun. Shortly turning right, there would only have been Rhydiau Bach, and turning left at the T-junction (where Siloh Manse now stands) nothing else had been built except Blaenrhyd, Ffynnonfach, and Blaencwm. All that area was then known as Sarn Fach, not Rhos, as it is now known. Several houses had been built on the Northern side of Rhos, Llangeler. These were the 'one-night' houses that had been built overnight. They simply consisted of four walls, only high enough to support the roof trusses. On top of these were branches covered with rushes or bracken, and a hole left in place of the chimney. If smoke appeared out of it before dawn, the dwelling could be claimed for ownership. The blacksmith would then be summoned to throw an axe in the four directions of the compass. Wherever the axe landed formed the boundary edge for the newly claimed territory. After a year or two, the little one-night house could be extended and improved and probably be rebuilt into a little two-roomed cottage or '*bwthyn*', as it was called. There would be a little attic upstairs, and the owner and his family would survive by keeping a cow or two on the Rhos.

Many of the 'one-night houses' were built around 1750: Penfforddnewydd, Bryn-noethwynt, Maespant, Bryneithin, Pencae, Pencaeau, Bwlchclawddbach, Pantbach, Penwaun, Rhydiau bach, Blaen-nant, Clais, and Penlon (where Gaerwennog now stands) just to name a few. The latter was occupied until 1930 by Mattie, who lived there on her own. She kept a couple of cows, and always used to smoke a pipe.

Because these dwellings were built on land owned by the Crown, people living in these houses had no legal rights. Indeed, it has often been overlooked that the people living in the 'one-night' houses were not the real owners. The land upon which the houses were built was crown property, and in 1848, when the crown land was sold, people living and extending the 'one-night' houses at their own expense found that they had to pay again for the ownership of their properties. There is documentary evidence attesting to this. For example, some of the tenants dwelling in these houses, and who had claimed a few acres of the common land nearby, had to pay 5/- rent annually for the land, as well as £60.00 to buy the house. In fact, the rights and privileges these people had enjoyed for over a hundred years was wiped out by one stroke of a pen.

During that time, a part of the moor was bought from the Crown to create the farm known as Rhosgeler. When the new owner of the farm began cultivating the land, building the hedges, and planting trees, he realised the hardship the people were having to endure by the loss of their grazing rights. Consequently, he gave back one nine and a half acre field to the people of Rhos, so that they could use it as they pleased – whether for recreation or grazing. But he put one clause into the agreement, and that clause stated that no-one could profit from the land. If any revenue was incurred, it was to go to the Parish Church of Llangeler to be distributed to the poor of Llangeler. This field is known to this day as 'cwmins', meaning common land.

In 1968, a large part of the moor was planted with conifers, and this destroyed the beauty of the open moor land. As I remember it, all of the moor land was treeless, apart from a few beech trees planted during the enclosure to create shelter for livestock. On the part of the moor familiar to me in my childhood, there are a few well-known springs (*'Ffynnonau'*). There was *ffynon Rhos,* also known as *ffynon Christmas.* People used to go and drink from it because it was supposed to have healing powers, but, to me, it tasted of iron and peat. On a Sunday evening, it was quite common to see several people tasting the water. Some would take a bottle home with them, probably to give to someone who was too ill or too old to come and fetch it for themselves. I am sure that several people believed that the water of *ffynon Rhos* could cure all ills. Further on can also be found the spring *ffynon Llanwrtyd,* also known as *ffynon Beca.* The third spring on the moor is *ffynon y Goelan Ddu,* nearly opposite the entrance to a farm called Hafod. Wells and springs were the main factors in deciding where a house or dwelling should be built, because it was essential to have a good supply of fresh water for people and animals.

Wells also played quite a large part in people's imaginations in Christian as well as in pre-Christian times. Beliefs in the magical powers of wells was so deeply rooted in the lives of people, that not even the Christian Church was able to eradicate them. The many sacred wells in many parts of the country, dedicated to patron saints were the destinations of pilgrimages. They were the holy wells, healing wells, wishing wells, and oracular wells. Indeed they preceded the holy wells in pagan times.

Here, I would like to quote from Edward Llwyd's '*Parochialia*' (D. Parry Jones, 1953, p.122) regarding the holy well of St Celer:

> *Not far from the church at the bottom of a steep hill issueth a fountain. Over the fall thereof, a little chapel is erected. Hither every summer, infirm people make a frequent resort, but particularly from the 21st of June to the feast of St Peter (29th) there will be such a concourse of people that no fair in Wales can equal it in multitude, out of an opinion that the saint endued it with such a virtue as will cure all infirmities. The tradition obtains that about two years since, some infirm persons left their crutches behind in the church in memory of their being cured by bathing in this well........In the churchyard there is a place which I may properly call a cemetery....where after bathing, the infirm*

must lie down to sleep, which as many do are persuaded will recover, otherwise not.

I will now return to my main theme where I was before I got carried away by the story about the holy well of St Celer.

On the highest point of the moor where the parish of Llangeler and Cynwyl Elfed meet, which is 310 metres above sea level, are three prehistoric monuments, namely Crug-glas, Crug-Bach, and Garn-Wen. These are stone-age burial places. They were constructed about the same time as the construction of the Egyptian pyramids, and indeed show many similarities to them: for instance, in the way the dead are buried, and in the way the construction was designed so that the sunlight at certain times of the year came through the entrance and fell on a wall and lit up a chamber in the tomb. The Trinity to the stone-age people were the sun, moon, and stars, and the importance of the sun and moon to these people is reflected in this construction. I have searched for Garn-Wen, knowing its position, but since the conifers have been planted, I can no longer find this important and ancient monument. Incidentally, the nearby farm of Triolmaengwyn ('*maen*' – stone, '*gwyn*' – white) is named because of its proximity to Garn-Wen.

About a mile East of these monuments is Carreg Hir, a long standing stone, eight feet tall (and probably an extra five or six feet of it buried in the ground) and about four feet wide. This single stone, in my opinion, is the only one left of a standing stone circle. All the others have probably been taken away and used by local farmers for gateposts during the time when the land was being enclosed – because I have seen many examples of such gateposts myself.

There is something about these long stones that fascinates me, and probably many other people. I am amazed when I stop and think about those people nearly four thousand years ago managing the most super-human task of transporting all those enormous stones from the Preseli mountains of Pembrokeshire to Stonehenge on Salisbury Plain in Wiltshire.

Once again, I turn away from Carreg Hir and I am reminded of an article in The Countryman, Spring, 1957, p.166 'Texts in Stone'. The article includes a photograph showing one of six boulders, inscribed with Biblical references, on the roadside, high above the Derbyshire village of Curbar. The inscriptions were carved in 1893 by Edward Gregory, a mole trapper from the Chatsworth estate. He was also an energetic local preacher and Sunday School teacher. He carved the inscriptions as a thank offering after recovering from a serious illness. Until his death, at the age of 85, he kept them clean and legible.

Near Carreg Hir is a farm called Blaenduad. About 1870, on a November moonlit night, the young wife of this farm was murdered by a single shot fired through the kitchen window. The bullet went through both her and the door to the dairy. Before she fell, she shouted 'He said he'd have me'. She had been preparing supper at the time, and she had people in the room with her. They witnessed it all, but there was nothing they could do. The murderer escaped on horseback across the moor, and a maid on a farm in the adjoining parish gave him an alibi – she said he was with her at the time of the murder. He was nevertheless arrested and tried in the court in Carmarthen. He was acquitted – probably because the trial was held in the English language, and local people were too afraid to testify. Had the trial been held in Welsh, the people would have felt more at home, and possibly would have spoken up. As a direct result, a family of considerable means became much poorer, and a couple of cottagers became well off.

The courts never heard what the unsworn juries discussed in the fields. But the local people knew who it was took his gun, which way he rode, and at what time he arrived in the adjoining parish. Although the accused was acquitted, he never slept again, and he always kept his gun within reach. He was, in fact, a brother to the young woman (who was murdered)'s husband, and there was, at one time, talk of a love triangle between the three. The question which occurs to me is, was he the murderer, or was it the husband who shot her? I think it was the latter.

Until the early and middle of the nineteenth century, agriculture and the woollen industry were the most important industries. After this time, several quarries were opened up to supply the stone for building purposes, and also to provide material for road construction, and so on, because transport was becoming increasingly important. I will talk about transport in more detail in subsequent chapters.

CHAPTER 3
Dwellings

Most of the farmhouse cottages as we know them in South West Wales were built at the end of the 1700's and during the first half of the 1800's.

These houses are typically long, low, two-storey buildings, with a central front door, and five symmetrically placed windows in the front wall. A long narrow room spans the back of the house, and there is a back door which usually opens at the side of the house. Very often, on the end of the house is a cart-house with a loft over it, with stone steps at the end of the house leading to the loft.

Each of these houses was usually built on, or near to, a site where a much older house used to be. We know this, because on some farms, the field nearest the house is sometimes called *Parc yr hen dŷ* (field of the old house). These original older houses had been built of stone and earth, having thatched roofs and earthen floors. They had had two or three rooms which were separated in the following manner: posts were driven into the ground and the walls constructed by plaiting willow or hazel between these posts – like a basket – and finally plastered with mud mixed with horse hair. Adjoining the house was a cowshed, and adjoining the cowshed was a stable. Access to the stable could be gained via an interconnecting door from the house. These old houses, although very primitive, were still a big improvement on the previous typical homes.

When people started to emerge from the Stone Age, leaving their caves in favour of some sort of house, the custom was to build a round pit which was then covered by some sort of cone shaped roof constructed of poles tied together and covered with leaf and bracken - the '*bwlchgylchoedd*' (round houses). This is not only the origin of the word '*bwthyn*' - the Welsh word for cottage - but also of the word 'booth' in the English language. The people were sometimes called 'pit dwellers'.

Manor houses of the Middle Ages were very simple in plan, only having one large room – The Great Hall – in which the owner, his family, his servants and his dogs all lived, dined, and slept. There was a log or peat fire on a hearth in the middle of this room, and the smoke emerged through a hole in the roof above. The fire was used for cooking and warmth. There was an earthen floor covered with rushes, and the windows were unglazed, and had wooden shutters. Progressive improvements included a raised floor, a private bedroom for the owner and his wife, and bedrooms for the members of his family and for guests. The fire place was moved to one wall instead of being in the middle of the floor, flues running up that wall to a chimney stack. One item of interest is that one little room was introduced which was called a 'solar' – a private room to be kept clean and tidy, and only to be used on very special occasions. This was something very like what we have today which we call the 'parlour', or in Welsh, *'y parlwr'*.

I well remember the *parlwr* when I was growing up – that it was a room whose door was always kept closed. Inside was a glass display cabinet where the best china was on show. There would be a table and chairs, and probably an oak linen cupboard. I always remember that the only time we children went in there was to brush our clothes before going to church. It is a room that smelt of Sunday – a place where you felt relaxed because of its charm and character – with its curtains crisp and bright, and the floor tiled in an unforgettable pattern of three different colours. I will never forget the peaceful atmosphere of that room.

It was not until almost the end of the Middle Ages that houses came to look more like the ones which are so familiar to us today. In the sixteenth century, the 'Great Hall' gave way to a smaller entrance hall – like we have now inside the front door – hence the word 'reception'. The various living rooms led off from this.

The next major change was the introduction of an upstairs. The staircase always led from the front hall, as it usually does today.

It was not until the beginning of the eighteen hundreds that there began a trend to build rural country cottages as comfortable dwellings. One characteristic of that time was the introduction of the sash window, which could be found in almost every house – although sash windows had been used for the big houses and mansions since the time of Christopher Wren.

I must admit here that some people, including myself, thought a cottage to be a single-storey house only, but a two-storey house, in some parts, is also called a cottage.

In this chapter I would also like to talk about some of the names of the houses and farmhouses in the locality. Blaensiedi, for example, is near the source of the river Siedi, '*blaen*' meaning 'at the beginning of'. Blaencwm is at the beginning of the '*cwm*' (valley). Ffynnonfach ('*ffynnon*' = well, '*fach*' = little) is near a small well.

There can be found a farm called Hafod (summer dwelling) in nearly every parish. (By the way, Hendre was a winter dwelling). The name Hafod derives from the ancient farm practice of turning out the cattle and sheep on to the high moor land to graze during the summer months. The children would take it in turns to shepherd these animals, and some of the older children would stop them wandering. Because some moor land reaches up to over a thousand feet above sea level, the weather can be very cold and wet, even during the summer months. So the shepherd, during the nice weather, would gather stones and timber and build a shack in which to shelter when the weather was rough. Subsequently, when the moor was enclosed, these shacks became farmhouses. A farm named Hafod is always found on the highest ground in the parish. Then there are names like Gwyddyl, Cilgynudd, Cilfforest and Cilblaidd, which have their origins in the Gaidelic or Irish

31

language. Much as we in Wales have Llan (church) at the beginning of many place names, in Ireland, the word for church is Kil, found in many Irish place names, such as Killarney, Kilorgan and many others. The only difference is that in Wales, the K is a C, because there is no K in the Welsh alphabet.

I will mention here some unusual names for dwellings in the locality. My guess is that Pelic, for example, was probably built by someone who had gone to sea, and served on Sir Francis Drake's flagship, *The Pelican* (subsequently renamed *The Golden Hind*). In our locality there can also be found houses called Calcut, Capadocia, and Salamanca. The reason for these names is probably because young men joined the militia to serve in far distant lands. When they retired and came home, they built houses and named them after some place that was memorable to them. The farm Blaenantrhys is probably named after Rhys ap Gruffydd who nearby had to submit to Henry 2nd in 1163.

A few people referred to the *rhos* (moor) as the *waun* (heath). This is the reason for the names Waunfawr and Penwaunfri - two farms on the moor. Again, Bwlchyddwyrhos means the gap between the two moors, because of its position between Penrhosfawr and

Penrhosfach ('head of the big moor', and 'head of the little moor' respectively).   There is also Garwen (*gaer*, fort, *wen*, white) because of its position near the Roman fort.

CHAPTER 4
The People

I will start with the people in general - I hope to say a little about individuals in later chapters.

Until about fifty years ago, the only language that was spoken in the parish of Llangeler, as in most parishes in West Wales, was Welsh. I think that the main reason for this was that large families existed which had been living in the same district for hundreds of years – there being no reason for them to uproot. Another factor was the landlord/tenant system, where succession from father to son over several generations was the norm. Probably we in West Wales are all descendants of New Stone Age Man – the Celts - who came to these islands from about 4500 to about 2500 BC. It was the Greeks who first wrote about them. The word 'Celt' seems to have some connection with 'forest' – probably because they had lived in the forests of Eastern Europe. When these people arrived in this country, they all spoke the same language, but gradually, as they migrated into different regions of the country, various dialects of the original language evolved. These dialects are now divided into two groups: the Gaidelic or Irish group, and the Brythonic or British group. In the Gaedelic group are Irish, Gaelic, and Manx, and in the Brythonic group are Welsh, Cornish, and Breton. The term 'Gaidal' survives in the Welsh language, *'Gwyddel'* meaning Irish man.

The Celts were tall muscular people with fair or red hair. They conquered the Iberians who were here before, simply because of their better weapons of bronze, with fine cutting edges. Once they had conquered the Iberians, they did not exterminate them, but used them as their slaves. Eventually the two races seem to have mixed, and in the course of time became a very powerful people known as the Silures – a people whom the Romans at a later date found great difficulty in subduing. (Morgan, 1909, p.98).

As I was saying, when I was young, Welsh was the only language spoken. During the war years I remember hearing, for the first time, other languages being spoken. This was because, at that time, German and Italian prisoners of war worked on most farms. When they spoke to us, they tried to speak in English, but when the spoke to each other they used their own language.

After the War, the estates gradually began to be sold, thus providing an opportunity for newcomers to move into the area. Prior to that, I had been able to walk across eleven adjoining farms from one to the next – and all the tenants had the surname 'Jones'. Today, only three of those eleven farms have their first language as Welsh, and only two have 'Jones's' in them. Thanks to the Celtic Brythonic race, Welsh is the oldest language in Europe. Unfortunately, it has been losing ground for many years, but the miracle is that it has survived at all – considering the knocks it has taken. In the Acts of Union of 1536 and 1542, it was officially banned: *'No person or persons that use the Welsh speech or language shall have or enjoy any Manner Office or Fees within this realm of England, Wales, or other the King's dominion'* (D Parry Jones, 1948, p.103). However, in the last forty years or so, I believe that there has been a reawakening of national awareness of the language, culture and history, and that it will be in the Welshman's thoughts and emotions for many generations to come. Welsh students and writers are more numerous today than ever before. Taking into account the many Welsh language classes that are available today, with excellent teachers dedicated to the teaching and preservation of the language, surely, that in itself, is a sign that the Welsh language will not die. When an old European language dies, surely it is a loss to civilization. In my opinion, it is better to preserve a living language than spend large amounts of money studying something that died out thousands of years ago.

One thing that is worthy of note is that there are pockets of Welsh speakers living in towns and cities in England, and there are flourishing Welsh places of worship and several influential groups of Welsh speaking people in these places who are proud of their culture.

I will end my discourse about the Welsh language now, but before I do so, I would like to mention my recollections of people coming to work on the Welsh farms as young boys from the Barnardo's homes. They came to farms where the farmer and his wife were almost illiterate as far as the English language was concerned. I remember my father saying that he remembered a neighbour, who had a young English lad working for him, trying to call him in for have a meal. What he said was 'Come to plat'. These young lads picked up the Welsh language extraordinarily quickly, and in twelve months had completely mastered the language as far as the daily work on the farm with its seasonal activities was concerned, and within two years they had the vocabulary of the average Welsh boy of their age, speaking it with very little trace of an accent.

Old Sayings and Traditions

In this part of the world, as in everywhere else, people had their own traditions and sayings. I will mention a few out of the sayings as they come to me:

- *'Bara i gi drwg'* - 'Bread to a sly dog'- meaning that if you came across someone you weren't sure was trustworthy, it was wise to do him a good turn.

- *'Os mis Mai oer a gwlyb y gawn, fenwent wâg a 'sgubor lawn'* – meaning that a cold wet May heralded a full barn and an empty graveyard.

- *'Bwrw glaw cyn saith, hundda cyn unarddeg'* - Rain before seven, fine before eleven. (This is not always true in my opinion).

- *'Glaw tonwyn Abertawe, tra bara'n dydd, fe bara ynte'* - Rain from Swansea, rain all day. In other words, rain from the South East lasts all day, whereas rain from the South West lasts for a few hours at a time.

- *'Niwl o'r mynydd, gwres ar y maesydd, niwl o'r mor, glaw ar ei ôl'* – Mountain mist heralds fine weather, but sea mist is a sure sign of rain.
- *Tra bor, fe bar'*- meaning while an animal eats, it will survive. (I think this goes without saying).
- *'Dyfal donc a dyr y garreg'* – Persist and the stone will break.
- *'Na werth dy iâr ar glaw'* – Don't sell your hen in when it's raining. In other words, make your animal look its best if you want to sell it.
- *'Os cynar canna'r gôg, gwerth dy geffyl a phryn dy bwn'* – If the cuckoo sings early, sell your horse and buy your sackful – i.e. reduce your stock and buy feedstuff. (Incidentally, the Welsh word for cuckoo is either *gôg* or '*gwcw*').
- *'Gwcw glame, cosyn dime'*. *'Glame'* falls on May 10th, *'Calan Mai'*. If you heard the cuckoo for the first time at that time - in other words, late, then you would have a *'cosyn dime'* - a ha'penny cheese – because there would be scarcity.

There are dozens of others, but I'll move on now to some of the traditions. Again, there are so many of them, it would take a whole book to include them all. Here are just a few:

- Cattle weren't brought in for wintering when their 'backs were wet'. In those days, when cattle overwintered in warm cowsheds, they wouldn't dry out properly when they sweated, especially with their thick winter coats. In this day and age cattle are kept during the winter months in airy cubicle sheds and yards, and they are free to go in and out at will. This means that this tradition is no longer relevant.

- Traditionally nothing was done to the animal - such as killing the pig, salting the meat, tail docking - when the moon was waning. These jobs had to wait until the waxing of the moon.

- The sowing of the oats took place between the twentieth of March and the sound of the first cuckoo. Oats sown after the arrival of the cuckoo wouldn't yield well.

Much depended on where you were when you heard the cuckoo for the first time in the Spring. If you happened to be in a lush field you would become well off, but if you were on bare ground, it would mean a hard year ahead financially. Also, if you were without money in your pocket, that's how you would be for the rest of the year. The worst misfortune befell those who heard it in bed, for it meant that during the course of the year, there would be much sickness and lying in bed.

There is a beautiful legend concerning the arrival of the cuckoo at St Brynach Church, Nevern, Pembrokeshire. The story goes that every year, on April 7th, when a mass is held dedicated to their Patron Saint, St. Brynach, (a saint of the sixth century), the service would never be commenced until the cuckoo had arrived and sang his song from the top of the famous stone dedicated to St Brynach, in the churchyard,. This stone, incidentally, stands at 13 feet high, and is one of the finest specimens of a Celtic Cross.

One year, the bird was late arriving, and the priest and the people waited patiently. After a long wait, the cuckoo came, settled on the stone, and started to sing. But the bird was so weak and worn out, that it fell and died. I can well imagine the poor bird's distress as it battled the storms raging over the Pyrenees, saying to itself 'I must get through. Tomorrow is St Brynach's Day, and I must be at Nevern. I have never failed before, neither did any of my ancestors - for our family for generations has been given the honour of starting the mass on this special day. I must not fail. I must not fail. Nor did it.

Another story that I'd like to share with you here is the dog rose legend (*Laura Foest, Summer 1957, p 268*):

> *My grandfather, a landscape gardener, told me this old Cornish story about the five sepals of the dog rose. There were five brothers, each of whom had a beard. When two of them decided to shave theirs off, one of the others was in doubt what he should do, for while the two with beards urged him to keep his, the others begged him to shave it off. Whichever advice he followed would not meet with general approval. At last he had an idea to please them all; he shaved off one side only. If you examine a dog rose you will usually find that little points grow on both sides of two of the sepals; two are without points and the fifth has them on one side only.*

I remember my father saying on many an occasion that the valley in the next parish always had either a thief or a shower in it. Then again, he said that if a grave was left open over a Sunday in

Ffynnon Henry's graveyard, there would be another funeral there before the following weekend. Then again, in some parts of the country there is a saying 'Open for a she, open for three'. The people in times past had noticed that if a female was buried, then two other funerals soon followed.

Country people sometimes had deep rooted beliefs and odd ideas which needed to be tolerated, however trying that was to their friends. I don't wish to be in any way critical when I say this, indeed I am quite admiring of their strong adherence to traditions and beliefs that had been handed down to them by their forefathers.

CHAPTER 5

The First Farmers

From the Neolithic or the New Stone Age – between the years 4500 and 2350 BC, most of the population were directly involved in farming and food production. Until that time people had been hunter-gatherers, but as the population increased, clearing and planting of the land, and the cultivation of crops took place. This led to a more reliable and abundant food source. Initially, planting took place on the same piece of ground until it was realised that this practice exhausted the land. So, further land was cleared, and the process repeated. Crops were usually of wheat and barley, and the forests gradually became replaced by a patchwork of small fields – the beginning of farming as we know it. Then came the domestication of the animals – sheep, pigs, pigs, cattle, goats and fowl. Tools were of stone – hence the term 'Stone Age Man' – their hammers, axes, and knives were all of stone, with wooden handles.

Man, it seems, may be the only animal to cook food before eating, so the ability to light a fire goes back far into the mists of time. Not only was fire used for cooking, it was also a source of heat during the evenings and cold winter months, and to deter predators such as wolves and other wild animals.

The most primitive method of lighting a fire was using friction to create heat. All that was needed was two pieces of wood to be rubbed together. One piece was held in one hand, and it was rubbed with another piece held in the other hand, in a sawing motion. This is known as a fire-saw.

Not only were they using fire to cook etc., but another important use for it was to light the beacons to warn other tribes. These beacons would always be on a very high vantage point - for example, on Rhos, Llangeler, probably at Crug-glas, where it could be seen from Glamorganshire in the South to Cardiganshire in the North.

While I'm on the subject of fire, I might as well add that there are many different legends as to the origin of fire. In Greek mythology someone brought a torch lit from the sun. The

Estonians thought that their God struck a stone with his heel and started a fire. And in Hindu mythology, thunder is the clatter of the sun horses' hooves in the sky. The Romans, Egyptians, Greeks, Persians, Aztecs and Peruvians all used to have a fire burning continuously in public buildings. If, for some reason that fire went out, all business was suspended until it was rekindled with some sort of ceremony. (Everyman's Encyclopaedia, 1978, vol. 5, p. 128).

CHAPTER 6

Their animals

The horse was domesticated as early as the Bronze Age, and formed the earliest type of the Welsh Mountain pony. During the Iron Age, the horse goddess Epona was worshipped – probably where the word pony stems from. Since then new breeds have been introduced by the Celts and Romans, and then the Normans with their large war horses. These were crossed with the native breeds, and, as a result, we have the cobs and shires which were adapted for pulling and for agricultural work, and the smallest breeds were used in the coal mines. (Everyman's Encyclopaedia, 1978, vol.6, p. 335). Until the seventeen hundreds, most of the agricultural work was done by oxen, before they were replaced by the horse.

Cattle have been domesticated from the Bronze Age - when they were used for pulling the plough and the harrow. Cows were also milked and used for beef, and their skins used for clothing. Cattle ownership meant wealth, and cattle were used as units of currency. White cattle were the sacred animals of the Druids.

Sheep were also domesticated by the early inhabitants of these islands - their meat for eating, and their skins important for warm winter wear, and to line dwellings.

Wild dogs and wolves were common, and it was from these that, with domestication and training, man's best friend emerged. Canine remains have been found alongside those of humans, dating back from over 3000 years BC. The Egyptians worshipped the dog. They in fact named a star Sirius, which was also known as the dog star because of its faithfulness in appearing at certain times to warn them of the approaching overflow of the Nile.

Over the years, dogs have been used for hunting and guarding properties, as well as pulling loads. According to an article by James E. Carver of Norfolk ('The Countryman' Winter 1957, p.791) at one time, as many as 20,000 dogs may have been used on draught work in Britain. Fish used to be brought from Southampton to London in small carts drawn by two or four dogs, with the driver sitting with his feet on the shaft. According to 'The

Countryman' (Winter 1957, p.791), Gertrude Jekyll, in her book 'Old West Surrey' says that the dogs were usually Newfoundlands, and that a team of four would carry four cwt. of fish. Dog transport was forbidden in the metropolitan area in 1840, and throughout the kingdom some fifteen years later.

Dogs nowadays are used for many different purposes, for example, by the army to detect explosives, by the police to detect drugs, and also the extraordinary guide dogs for the blind. Whenever I see a blind person being led by a guide dog, I have to stop and marvel at the closeness binding the two together. I remember listening to the radio many years ago. It was 1958 was called 'Have a Go', and the compère was Wilfred Pickles. He would introduce each contestant to inform his listeners. One contestant still remains in my memory. Wilfred Pickles said, 'My next contestant is a blind lady with her guide dog'. He chatted to her for a while before he asked her whether she had any wish she would like granted. This was her reply: 'I only wish that my dog Judy will live as long as I do'. I will never forget that answer – I expected her to say she wished to have her sight back. Her faithful companion was more important to her for reasons I will probably never understand.

When I think about the people who first domesticated wild animals, I think they must have been quite adventurous to try to catch them and tame them. It must have taken many hundreds of years of breeding and selection. It was not just the animals that were changing – it was the people as well.

CHAPTER 7

The Romans and Early Christianity

Before I start speaking about the Romans, I would like to include the legend about Brut the Trojan. This story was told by John James, Waunfawr, the famous hermit of these parts. John was a man who lived without a calendar or clock, and who was drawn back to live as they did in the Stone Age. For someone who hadn't had much education and lived an isolated life, he was remarkably knowledgeable, and had his own philosophy. He said that around the 13th century BC, a Trojan by the name of Brut or Brutus conquered these islands (namely England, Scotland and Wales), and named it Britannia. He married Innogen, and had three sons named Locrinus, Albanicus, and Camber. After Brut's death, Locrinus became the king of England, and named it Lloeger (the Welsh word for England) after his own name. Albanicus became king of Scotland – hence the Welsh 'Yr Alban' meaning Scotland, and Camber became king of Wales – which thus became Cymru (Welsh for Wales).

The invasion of Britain by the Romans, took place somewhere between 43 and 47A.D. There seemed to be a large Roman military presence in Wales alone. It is estimated that, at one time, there were about 30,000 troops here, and they remained here for over 300 years until Magnus Maximus had to remove them to mainland Europe to deal with uprisings. Incidentally, Magnus Maximus was the last Roman leader in Wales, and was credited with freeing Wales from the Romans.

The main feature of the Roman occupation was its military character – mainly shown in their forts or camps, and the splendid road system connecting them. When they moved their armies from one camp to another, the Romans moved in a straight line from A to B. This was very unlike the New Stone Age people who always moved along ridges from one vantage point to the next – very much like cattle or sheep, moving with the terrain, not against it.

The two main Roman roads in the county of Carmarthen were named after the famous governor in Britain, Julius Frontinus. One road was Via Julia Maritima, a coastal road, and the other was Via Julia Montana which came over the mountains. These two roads converged near a place called Pensarn near Carmarthen (which the

Romans called Maridinum). The word '*sarn*' means lane or narrow road, and from Pensarn, a Roman road or lane, known as Sarn Helen, branched off – probably towards Llandeilo and the gold mines of Dolaucothi. From these roads another one crossed towards the Preseli mountains – crossing the parish of Llangeler by way of Blaenant Rhys, past Bwlchyddwyrhos, then between Blaenshedi and Glyncoch, then between Trialmawr and Glynllwyd. From there it climbs towards the fort between the two farms Gaerwenuchaf and Gaerwenisaf ('*Caer*': fort, '*uchaf*': above, '*isaf*': below). Sarn Helen can again be traced near Penboyr Church and at Bwlchydomen before crossing into the parish of Cilrhedyn on its way towards the Preseli mountains. In the parish of Llangeler, Sarn Helen, much later on, was known as The Coaches Road – probably because that was its use long after the Romans left.

Long before and during the time that the Romans were here, the weather was much warmer (it has gradually been cooling ever since) - ideal for vineyards and wine making, which the Romans practised. The Romans also introduced us to new crops – apples, carrots, turnips, parsnips, leeks, cherries, etc.

Early Christianity came to this country during the second century A.D. at a time when trading between the Celts and Gaul was brisk. Trade in tin and copper had already been long established, and there were well established trade routes between Britain and France, and between Britain and the shores of the Mediterranean Sea. Since there were Christian churches in these places, it is quite probable that Christianity travelled along the trade routes, or, on the other hand, it may have come by accident, or through missionary work. What is certain, however, is that the excellent road system created by the Romans helped the spread of Christianity.

Until this time, Druidism seems to have been the only religion. The Druids were priests and bards, and the Druidic order had been around since time immemorial. Human sacrifices and religious practices had been taking place in oak groves. The oak tree was sacred, and mistletoe was used in one of their religious ceremonies. Druidism and Christianity seem to have flourished side by side for a long time, and mistletoe is still brought into the house at Christmas time.

The Druid Trinity consisted of the sun, moon, and stars – unlike the Christian Trinity, and there were several Druid Gods (polytheism), such as a God of the Rain, a God of the Wind, and a God of the Wells, where worshipping took place. Christians adopted this practice, and several became holy and wishing wells, where people sacrificed their coins. Christianity, in its most highly evolved form, had only one God (monotheism).

In a way, the Roman invasion came about the same time as early Christianity to this country. Nobody can be quite sure how many people were involved with carrying Christianity here - it certainly was more than one person. I like to believe what I was taught at school, which is as follows: Joseph of Aramathea was the person who brought Christianity to this country at about this time. The legend goes that he arrived at Glastonbury, and is supposed to have put his stick in the ground there. The stick took root and grew, and became known as the tree of Joseph, also known as the Glastonbury thorn.

After the Romans left Britain, the country fell into the Dark Ages – a period which lasted several hundred years. It was during this time (between 660 and 770) that the Anglo Saxons – who had already settled in England – began engaging in conflict with Wales. This came to a head when Harold Godwinson, Earl of Wessex, took over parts of Wales.

CHAPTER 8
The Drift from the Land

Until the onset of the iron works and coal mines in South Wales, agriculture was the main industry - food being so essential a commodity. So, for many thousands of years, from the beginning of farming until the 18th century, nearly everyone worked on the land. It is true that by this time, a few men were needed in the building trade, and for quarrying etc. But by the end of the 19th century the number of miners in the coal fields of South Wales was almost 300,000, not including the men working in the steel and iron works.

Before the drift of labourers from West Wales to the coal mines, iron and steel works (and to a lesser extent copper and tin works), about 90% of men worked on the land. But by about 1912, that figure had dropped to about 10%. The young men would earn much more than they would have done working on the farms, and the hours were not as long. Moreover, they worked together in groups, not in isolation as they would have been doing had they been ploughing or shepherding – although, in my experience, there was intermittent community work where there would have been plenty of company and fun, not as it is today where farmers work in isolation. It is quite normal these days for a man to spend twelve or fourteen hours in a tractor cab, and be on his own for days at a time with no-one with whom he can talk.

It seemed at the time as though the coal mines were opening up and swallowing the country's population in their thousands. Shorter hours and bigger pay packets drew the young workers from the farms, and there was mass migration from West Wales to the valleys. However, although the coal mines gave generously - providing gold watches and chains - they also took without pity or remorse. When I was young, I used to hear my parents mention names of men who had been killed or injured in the coal mines. That used to prey on my mind every time I travelled towards South Carmarthenshire: Cross Hands, Drefach, Cefn Eithin, Cwmmawr, Tumble, and seeing - what they used to call - the coal tips. They were, in fact, large mounds composed of the waste from the mines that could not be used. Statistically, between 1840 and 1920, one miner on average was killed every six hours, and one injured every two minutes.

In Aberfan, Merthyr Vale, on the 21st of October, 1966, one of these tips moved down the side of the mountain, burying the school and twenty houses. 144 people lost their lives – 116 of them were children under the age of 10. In coalmining communities, disasters normally injured or killed fathers or brothers, but in the Aberfan disaster, it was the children who were killed.

As well as in the industrial parts of South Wales, work was to be found in the building of the railways, and all that that encompassed - for example, in the levelling the ground, in building embankments, blasting through cuttings, laying the lines, building the railways, not to mention tunnelling. I will be mentioning the railways again in a later chapter.

CHAPTER 9
My Childhood Memories

In this chapter I will describe what it felt like growing up in a rural community in West Wales. I was born in 1940, at the beginning of the Second World War. I will share my memories of the war years separately at the end of this chapter. There was no such thing as class distinction as to whether the children came from farms or cottages, nor as to whether they attended church or chapel. Everyone was equal, and the only language spoken was Welsh. Every child in our district went to the same school. We all knew about each other, and played the same games. Sunday was the only day of the week when there was some restriction on what we were allowed to do. On that day, no-one was allowed to use a pocket knife to cut wood, and no-one was allowed to whistle. In those days, Sunday was a day of rest for man and beast. The worship of God was the most important duty on this sacred day.

Although I grew up in a home that is nearly half a mile from the nearest neighbouring farm, I can't remember feeling lonely.

Sometimes on Saturdays, school friends not living on farms would come and spend the day with us to play and explore. As soon as we were old enough, we had to brush the yard first – then we would be free to play all day. During the summer, when the weather was warm, we spent most of our time playing by the pond – which was about 25 yards both in width and length, and about four feet deep. It was where the water was stored to turn the water wheel, and was the favourite place of our ducks and geese. I remember how we used to entice the dogs into the pond and watch them swim across. Then they would come out and shake themselves all over us. Sometimes we would take off our boots and socks, and paddle into the centre – it was all short trousers in those days.

Me with my brother, Gwynoro

In the winter, when the pond was frozen, we would skate. Also, we played '*cylch*' with an iron hoop, which was about 18 – 24 inches in diameter. The hoop was pushed with a metal rod made for the purpose, and bent at the end to fit the hoop. We would run and play this game for hours. Because both the hoop and the handle were made from steel, you can imagine the high-pitched tone that could be heard, especially with three or four going together on the same yard, and, in addition, the noise of the steel hoops banging against the stones on the yard and the lane.

Nowadays, on wet days, children largely stay in the house and watch television. In those days, we only came into the house for meals. If it was wet, we went into the barn, where we played on the see-saw (a plank of wood over a wooden barrel) or the swing (constructed from a stout rope tied to the beams). We also played with a whip and top, and hide and seek. Our favourite place for this was in the '*ydlan*' – the stack yard – where there were plenty of corn stacks ('*helem*', pl. '*helmi*') providing ideal hiding places. Another favourite was rounders.

After tea, which was around four o'clock, it was time to help with the chores: fetching clean water from the well ('*ffynnon*'), bringing in firewood, collecting the eggs, and go and fetch the cows in the summer months. At other times we might be asked to fetch potatoes from the field – if it happened to be the time of the year when the potatoes hadn't yet been lifted. Whilst on the subject of potatoes, during the big day of the potato harvest in the autumn, we would be kept home from school to help with the work.

At the end of the summer, one very exciting task was to pick hazel nuts (*'cnaio'* – *'cnai'*= nuts). On the farm there are endless hedges and woodlands with a large quantity of hazel trees. We used to pick sacks full of nuts and remove the green leaves in the evenings. A couple of sacks would then be hung above the fireplace to keep warm, to be eaten during the winter months. By this time, they tasted very sweet. By the way, when nut collecting, whoever found a patch of bushes laden with nuts could shout and claim the patch – no-one else was allowed to pick there!

In those days, nobody wore wellingtons. Footwear was either clogs or boots for school, and shoes for special occasions (such as trips or visiting relatives) and to wear on Sundays. I remember when it was time for a new pair, my father would cut a thin stick – about the thickness of a pencil – and tell me to take off my boots.

He would then measure my foot length, and to that length would add the length of a grain of barley. He the cut the stick to that length, and when he went to the cobbler or the market in Carmarthen, he would choose a pair of boots or clogs that fitted the stick. It was not until I was ready to leave school that I tried on a pair of boots for myself.

From time to time during play at school (and bear in mind that we walked a round trip of five miles every day to school and back) we would lose a plate '*pedol*' (horse shoe). I should explain that on the heel of a clog was miniature horse shoe, and on the sole was a larger version. Sometimes these would become loose, lost, or worn. When that happened, I was instructed to call at Glaspant, the home of the local cobbler, to have it repaired – because walking home all that way without the 'shoe' would soon wear out the sole or heel.

Listening to my parents' accounts of their own younger days, I had the impression that things hadn't changed very much from one generation to the next.

I have memories of going on errands to adjoining farms, and walking across fields, through woods and crossing streams. If I was following a path, there would be a '*bontbren*' or footbridge crossing the stream. Other times I had to take or fetch something to or from the blacksmith. Usually I was asked to do this on a Saturday morning or during the school holidays. I would probably meet other children on my way. One Saturday I remember well was when I had been asked to meet someone out on the main road and deliver some message or other. On the way home, I met one of the boys from school who had been on an errand to fetch eggs from his Aunty. I decided to ride my bike straight at him as a joke, and swerve at the last minute. Unfortunately, he saw me coming, and also swerved – to the same side as me! We both ended up on the ground on top of the bike, and all the eggs were broken. He ran home to tell his mother what I had done. Needless to say, I was told to replace the loss with another dozen eggs that same day. This I did, after I had been home to face the music. Incidentally, from that day on, this boy and I have been the best of friends to this day.

Some of the things we did were not very safe, and would not have passed today's more rigorous safety requirements. One example would have been the sling we made. This was a stick, about a yard long, with a slot at one end. There we placed a stone, about the size of a pullet's egg, and by holding the stick at the other end, we could throw the stone over a hundred yards without much effort.

Another thing we made to play with required goose quills. We collected these when the geese shed their feathers, then cut off the pointed end as well as the other feathery end, leaving the shaft of the feather. This was our gun. Then we made a wooden ramrod to fit the 'gun', about 1/4″ shorter than its length. A slice of potato, about 1/4″ thick could then be inserted into the makeshift 'gun', and fired by using the ramrod. This technique could also be employed using an elder stick, about 9″ long, and removing the pith to make the shaft. Instead of potato, I remember we used chewed paper which had dried and become hard. This was inserted about ¾ of the way into the shaft, then another wet piece of paper would be rammed on top of it, using the ramrod. Doing this created pressure within the tube, until the dried piece of paper exploded out of the other end of the tube with a loud and satisfying bang.

Another game was 'pitch in' where we would make a sling out of a willow branch and elastic, and sling stones. These games were very dangerous when I think of it now, but I can't remember anyone being injured by them.

There is one last memory to share with you before I finish this chapter. It's how we made whistles out of sycamore – these trees grew abundantly on our farm. We required a sycamore stick about the thickness of my thumb, and about six inches long with no notches or flaws. This stick was sucked by mouth for about a minute, and the soaked bark was then tapped to loosen it so that it could be removed. After removing the bark, a slot was cut in the wood, and the bark replaced. When blown, a high pitched whistle ensued.

I will now mention my memories of the war years. I remember the blackouts, gas masks, ration books, and the evacuees. I remember carrying my gas mask to school, and I can recall seeing the arrival of the land girls.

The Women's Land Army was first founded in 1917 under the directorship of Dame Muriel Talbot. Over 18,000 women and girls were enrolled to do all kinds of work – agricultural, horticultural, and forestry, during the First World War. During the Second World War, nearly 80,000 girls volunteered to work in the Women's Land Army. It was disbanded on 30th November, 1950.

Also, I well remember the first time I saw POW's coming to work on the farms. The first were Italian, and later, German. They were billeted at Henllan camp, were dropped off by lorry in the mornings, and picked up in the evenings. These prisoners were treated well – when they came to work on the farms, for instance, they always ate with the family at the same table. After all, it was not the common man who was responsible for sowing the seeds of war, but it was young men who had to reap the harvest that the so-called leaders had sown.

I was too young to realise the heartache and worry that families had to endure by the absence of loved ones who had joined up to go to war. I do remember the welcome home parties and concerts after the war ended. At the time, I didn't realise that it must have been the great relief of a happy reunion, but for others a very sad time when the loved ones did not return. I remember my parents and others recalling their memories of the First World War. My father was one of five brothers who served in the Great War. At the same time, one of his sisters, my Aunty Mary, served as a nurse in the Red Cross. All of them came back alive, although two were wounded. My father suffered for the rest of his life from the effects of being gassed.

There seem to have always been wars, but they were fought in far distant lands – for example, the Crimean War and the South African Boer Wars, just to name a couple. In the 'old days' every parish had to make sure that four young men were available to join the army or militia, as they were called in those days. But often, young men would join up of their own free will. Some parents were too frightened to allow their sons go to the fairs on their own, in case they would be attracted by the scarlet coats of the soldiers, and take the Queen's shilling – which automatically meant they had joined the army. In the 'old days' it was not considered respectable to join the army, for a soldier was looked upon as somewhat suspicious, and not to be trusted. But during the First World War, when soldiers became so common, there was a change of attitude. From then on, the soldier was admired and respected as someone who defended their country against the enemy.

In the following chapters, I hope to recall some of the way of life that has gone forever. The change has been so rapid, it has even taken place during my own lifetime. Anyone under the age of fifty won't remember seeing a rick of sheaves being built and thatched, seeing a gambo with a hay loader behind it picking up loose hay, a pair of horses pulling a binder, or a cow being milked by hand with the milker sitting on a three-legged stool with a tin bucket between the knees. All these scenes have gone forever.

CHAPTER 10
My School Days

When I look back on my school days, and my recollections of my parents' conversations about their school days, I realise how lucky we were. I am aware that when both my parents went to school they were encouraged to speak in English – which was very difficult for them, because until they started school, they hadn't heard a word of English. When my great grandparents started school it was even harder because at that time, the 'Welsh knot' held a reign of terror. The 'Welsh knot' was a piece of wood with a piece of string attached to it so that it could be hung around the neck. If a child was heard using a Welsh word, the 'Welsh knot' would be given to the child to wear. As soon as another child was heard speaking Welsh, it would be transferred to that child. Whoever was wearing it at the end of the day would be punished - by a flogging, or in some schools suspended from the rafters in a basket, or sometimes made to stand on a bench holding a heavy bible in one hand. In parts of North Wales, instead of wood, slate was used, and it was termed the 'Welsh stick'. These forms of punishment were common in those days. For instance, in a Quaker school at Sidcot, a boy making a serious grammatical error was punished by fastening a small log (a 'grammarlog') to his leg. It was worn until some other boy made a mistake, when the log would be handed over to him (D. Parry Jones, 1964, p.150).

I started school, like everyone else, at the age of five at Brynsaron School. Everyone walked to school – there were no school buses at the time. Speaking of buses, there were several buses on the main road running between Carmarthen and Cardigan. The bus company was the Western Welsh, and the buses ran on the hour at Groesffordd, designed to connect with the Newquay – the bus that ran through Llandysul. So, if we wanted to catch a bus down towards Newcastle Emlyn, we had to be at the St James junction at five minutes to the hour, and if we wanted a bus to Carmarthen, we needed to be there at five past the hour. It was a very good service – it ran every day of the week, and the buses were nearly full because there were not many cars on the road in those days. After about 1952, double deckers ran most of the time. But back to my walk to school. This was a two and a half mile walk. I was the youngest of four, so I had to keep up. Before we had reached the main road, the group of children had swelled to over a dozen, and yet more joined on the way down the main road. And by the time we had reached our destination, our numbers comprised half of the total number of children at school. The other half came from the opposite direction – from Saron and Pentrecwrt. In those days, Welsh was the only language you would hear. Another thing I should mention is that, unless it was very, very wet or cold, the front door of every house I passed was open, and probably the kettle singing on the fire. In those days, people didn't bother to knock – they just shouted 'Hello!' and walked in – they could be certain of a warm reception and hospitality.

Miss Evans was the infants' teacher. Because we had a long walk to school, and our clothes were often wet, Miss Evans would have us stand by the fire until we were dry. After being in school a few days, she would make a long card for each child with their full name at the top, so that they could practise reading and writing it. When children could write their name on the blackboard without copying it from the paper, she would have a little ceremony as a reward. All the children would gather round to watch her cutting up the card and putting it in the fire or in the bin. Miss Evans had been the only infants' teacher there long before my time, and continued to be long after I left there.

The middle classroom had several different teachers during my time there, but the biggest shock I had was when I went to the Headmaster's class. The master was a Mr Jones: he carried a stick and shouted for silence. I had never heard the word before, and didn't know what it meant – but I soon found out! Mr Jones retired during the time I was in his class. He had a good baritone voice, and also played the violin - and accompanied us when we were singing. Every morning we had to sing the French National Anthem! I'll never know why we had to sing the French National Anthem in English in a Welsh school. During my last year at Brynsaron School, Mr Davies, Woodlands, was the Headmaster.

The walk home from school was a time when we didn't have to worry that the bell was going to ring. On the main road, the first house we came across was 'Wenallt', and opposite it was a pill-box having a back access where we sometimes hid and pretended to shout through the shutters. One morning, on the way to school, we had a big disappointment – some German POW's were demolishing our hideout with sledgehammers and bars. The war was now over, and there was no need for the pill-box any more, so that was the end of our pill-box.

After 'Maesyrhaf' (formerly ''Penffosddu' where my great grandmother grew up) we came to The Lamb Inn, kept at that time by Tom and Rachel. At that time, The Lamb was a little farm as well, where they kept a few cows. The cowshed and barn were near the road, with a little hayshed behind them – where the car park is situated now.

Next was 'Ty Isaf' which had a post office, and a little further on were a grocer's shop and a cobbler's. The cobbler would make our clogs, and also repair them if necessary on our way home. Opposite 'Glaspant' (where the shop was) was the only water tap that I knew of, and on a hot summer's day, it was a blessing.

Near 'Glaspant' were two roads branching off, and some of the children departed on these. By the time we reached St James' church, we left the group and turned towards home, leaving the rest to carry on towards 'Tycoch' and their homes.

After turning off at St James', on our right was a field called 'cwmins' (common) – a favourite camping ground for gypsies. There was one particular family of Romany gypsies called 'the Hurns', comprising the mother and father, a son called Merlin and a daughter called Sheila. They used to come over to our farm and play with us during the school holidays. They never went to school themselves, but went round the farms and houses with their parents selling baskets and clothes pegs, and anything else they had made themselves. I remember Mrs Hurn for her long black hair made shiny with soapy water, and all the shining copper and brass pots and pans. Their caravan was beautifully painted in red and green. They had hens (mostly bantams), dogs, and of course, three or four piebald horses grazing the heather and bog grass growing in '*cwmins*'.

Many years later, when I was an adult, Merlin came here to see me. He was then living in Pembrokeshire, and he told me that Sheila had married and was living in Ireland. It was then that he told me that he and his sister had learned to read, being taught by Mrs Blodwen Jenkins who had lived in 'Bancymeillion' near St James' church.

Continuing on our way home, after passing 'Bryn' chapel, we came to another chapel called 'Siloh'. When I come to think of it now, there were two chapels and a church within a stone's throw of each other. Just before Siloh, there was the '*Mans*' where the minister lived. At that time, it was the Rev Derfel Rees. Beyond the chapel was 'Brynglas', wher Jams the carpenter lived. And if I had turned down on my left, opposite the '*Mans*' and walked for about fifty yards, I would have come to the blacksmith's shop. We could hear his hammer and anvil from a long way off.

Further on again, we passed 'Glasfryn', then 'Brynteg' where John lived. He was the 'lengthman' for the County Council, taking care of the roads in winter – keeping the ditches open, or repairing the hedges and walls, and in the summer, keeping the hedges cut and tidy, and keeping the verges like lawns with his sickle and scythe. We used to pass him nearly every day. After John retired, William Jones 'Pelican' took over. He was a hard worker, like John, and kept the roads and lanes tidy until machinery began to be used. William was one of the people who used to plant a couple of rows of potatoes in one of our fields (see later on in this script).

Next on our left was 'Ffynnonfach' where more children would leave the group. In fact, nearly every house that we passed, was the destination for some child or children – they had reached home. I used to envy the children living near the school, especially during the homeward journey in hot weather, because we were tired and hungry. In the mornings it wasn't as bad, because we were fresh and fed. It was the homeward journey that was draining our energy.

Sometimes during the summer we took what we called a 'short cut' home from school. It wasn't really a short cut, but it was a change. We took the lane below the school, past the entrances to 'Mountain Hall' and 'Cilgynudd' until we reached 'Cwmrhyd'. There we climbed the hill until we reached the lane into 'Tyhên', then through the field until we crossed the stream by 'Gwarcwm'. There we had a choice of going up 'Triolbach' lane or 'Gwarcwm' lane until we had reached the normal route.

When we were eleven or twelve years' old, we had the opportunity to take the 'scholarship' as it was then called (the equivalent of the 'eleven plus'). My two sisters took the exam, and both went to the Grammar School. But my brother and I decided to go to Henllan Secondary Modern School instead.

Henllan School consisted of a converted old prisoners-of-war camp. This had been built during the war, to hold first Italian prisoners, and later German prisoners. Most of the huts were built of reinforced concrete panels, but some of the first ones were of felt and wood. The only brick built building was the old hospital block which was converted into the science block. I had to catch the Clarke bus to Henllan at St James' – the bus came over the top from Capel Iwan. When I look back at my time in Henllan, I have fond memories of several of the teachers and also of the children, some of whom I still see from time to time.

Form 1A with Mr Thomas as form master

Amongst some of the teachers I remember well was Jimmy Thomas. He took English and Religious Instruction, at both of which he was excellent. On Sundays he was a Lay Reader. Then there was Mr James who taught History and Geography – my favourite subjects. Mr Elias taught woodwork, Mr Lewis, games and Art, Jack Evans, gardening, Miss John, music, Miss Arwyn, Welsh, Mr Llewelyn, science, and his wife, Mrs Llewelyn, Maths. By the way, they married during the time I was in Henllan. There was also Mr Williams who taught English, and I must not forget Mr J Tysul Jones, the Headmaster. I should also mention the caretaker, Mr Evans, who lit the stoves every morning in every classroom, because in the middle of every hut was a stove with a pipe rising and emerging through the roof. If you were near the stove, you would roast, and if you sat at the front or back, you would freeze!

Although there is not much left of Henllan School as I remember it, the hut that the Italian POW's converted into a Roman Catholic church is still standing. During their spare time, when they were not working on the farms, these POW's converted the hut into a place of worship for themselves. They stacked empty National dried milk tins, plastering them with plaster of Paris to replicate columns, probably similar to the columns in their Italian churches back at home. They also constructed an altar, and above the altar one of the prisoners, a Mario Ferlito, painted a mural of The Last

Supper. Considering it was war time, and it was difficult to obtain almost anything, the POW's set about boiling different parts of plants to extract the natural colours, and use these as different coloured paints. Bronwydd Mansion at the time was falling into disrepair, and they used the bell for their church. It was put on the roof of the hut, so that it could be rung before every service. It was obviously very important to them to have a sacred place to worship in their own language, although they were prisoners of war, and far from home.

The altar at P.O.W. Church, Henllan *(photograph by kind permission of the Thomson family, Henllan)*

It seems to be that whenever people find themselves in exile, no matter from what country, they group together and seem to create part of their homeland. It was important to the Welsh people who settled in Patagonia, for instance, to immediately build a chapel to worship in Welsh on a Sunday.

A few years after I left Henllan School, a new school opened at Newcastle Emlyn to take its place.

In the next section, I will be talking about something completely different - the traditional farm practices during the year. To do justice to this section, I think I will divide it up according to the four seasons – Spring, Summer, Autumn and Winter. I will give an account of what I remember, and also an account of what my parents and grandparents passed on.

CHAPTER 11

Springtime

I think it best to start on the first day of Spring – about the middle of March, when the days and nights are of equal length.

During March, ploughing would have to be finished. Some of the ploughing would have already been done in the Autumn, when a stubble field would have been ploughed ready for the potatoes and green crops for the following year - this was to give the winter frosts a chance to break up the soil.

Ploughing with three horses

(Voysey collection, MERL, University of Reading)

The plough is indeed one of the oldest implements used in husbandry. It has been in use for thousands of years, ever since man started growing crops – albeit in a very primitive form made from wood. At first ploughs were pulled by oxen or buffalo, and this practice still exists in some countries today. But since the early eighteen hundreds, most of the ploughing has been done by horses – usually in pairs. On some farms, however, they would use three, especially if they were using a two-furrowed plough which was useful on light soil. On stony ground a one-furrowed plough was more practical.

During the Second World War tractors began to appear on our fields. One farmer out of ten had a tractor by 1942, and by 1948, when the grey Ferguson arrived, nearly every farm had a tractor. Steam tractors had been around before 1880. In 1889, the American Burger tractor appeared in the Midwest, powered by an internal combustion engine – which took over from the steam tractors. It was the food crisis of 1916 that opened up the market for the first tractors that became so common on our fields.

The horse plough was about the only important implement which could not be converted to fit the tractor, so when the new tractor came, a new plough came as well – usually two- or three-furrowed. The harrows, binder, mower, rake, and even the gambo and the tub cart could be converted to be pulled by the tractor.

The main part of the horse-drawn plough was the frame or beam. To this, the handles were attached, and also the frame to hold the mould board or 'casting' which turned the soil. At the front of the casting, the share was attached – it was called the '*swch*'. At the front of the beam, there was what we call '*y clust*'. To this the '*cambren*' – the swingle tree - was attached, connecting the plough to the team of horses.

When starting a field, the first job was to mark out the headland (or '*talar*'). This was usually seven yards wide. It was done by measuring from the hedge, then marking it out with a thin stick, roughly every sixty yards. A thin shallow furrow was then turned going from one mark to the next. This was called '*y mwidin*' or scrap and that marked the headland. Then the whole field was ploughed, and finally the headland.

On very hilly ground, ploughing was done one way only. By this I mean the ploughing was done on the way down, travelling up empty, or '*gwag*' – i.e. without ploughing. On land that was not too hilly, however, ploughing could be done in both directions - this was the most common method of ploughing. Incidentally, the plough always turns a furrow to the right. Ploughing would start near the middle of the field and a straight furrow cut. Then a furrow would be made on the way back - parallel with the first, so that the sod would fall exactly touching the first, but not overlapping it. The ploughman would then work up and down –

cutting furrows parallel with these two original furrows. He worked in circles in this way, always turning right, but did not use the plough at the far and near (headland) edges. When that entire piece of the field had been ploughed, it was called a back ('*cefn*'). Then the rest of the field could be tackled. This was called the '*grwn*' (the round). The first furrow would be cut parallel to the original first furrow, and the ploughman would work again in a circular fashion, always turning left this time, ploughing on the way up and down, working towards the middle of the '*grwn*'.

Turning the last furrow in the field

(Hulton archives - Getty Images, Bayham Street, London)

89

I think this method was employed not to waste any time travelling too far on the headlands, because that was when the plough was being transported, not used. When the field was subsequently harrowed, it resulted in a flat turned field. If there were any flaws, on the following year the first furrow would be in a different place. Obviously, in a very big field, there would be more than one '*cefn*'. Of course there were also the 'reversible ploughs' which could be adjusted to turn the sod in either direction, but they were more suitable for flat land.

As a matter of interest, the first Monday after Epiphany in some parts of England was called Plough Monday, as a reminder that the ploughing season was about to start.

The basic design of the plough has not changed appreciably since before the Roman invasion. It still turns the soil in the same way helped by a cutter ('*cwlltwr*') – a metal disc attached separately in front of the ploughshare. This makes an initial cut along which the share can travel. On some of the horse ploughs, the '*cwlltwr*' was just a blade bolted on to the beam.

The first tractor-drawn ploughs were called trailer ploughs, but as soon as the hydraulic system became standard in some tractors, the hydraulic ploughs appeared. These were very popular: one reason for this was that they could be lifted and reversed back into corners or awkward places.

After ploughing, the fields were left for the furrows to dry out before harrowing:

Harrowing with a zig zag harrow

(MERL collection, University of Reading)

If the ground was dry enough, oats would be sown any time after 20th March, unlike barley which would be sown towards the end of April, in case of frost. In this part of Wales, wheat is not ideal because of the cold, wet weather. The fields were cropped in rotation: first hay on grassland, then oats for two years, then potatoes and green crops such as mangolds, kale and sweeds, then the following year, barley, undersown with grass seeds ready for the hay harvest the following year. There were two ways to sow corn – by hand or by drill. My father always sowed by hand, in fact, two hands. He used to have a tub strapped to his shoulders leaving his hands free to throw – with the right hand to the left and with the left hand to the right.

As soon as the oats were sown, the potato field was ploughed for the second time (having been left to dry after the first ploughing) to open the rows. Nowadays, potatoes are planted using the tractor, but when I was young, it was all done using a horse and a one row ridger. The common name for it was a 'double tom'. It had two mould boards instead of the metal cutting edge of the plough. The mould boards turned the earth both to the right and left, so it was effective in creating a furrow for the potatoes.

After opening the rows, the next task was to take out the farmyard manure. This was stored during the winter months - supplied from the stable, calf pens and cowsheds. It was taken out by horse and tub cart. Whoever made tub carts made them all the same. The volume would be one cubic yard, there was a fitting on the front called a 'standard' which would have six apertures allowing the tub to be tipped in six different positions for unloading the manure. The tailboard ('*caead*') could be removed out of the way.

It was usually one long hard day's work to manure the ground for the potatoes, and the following day, they were planted. It was the usual custom that families who lived in local cottages could plant a few rows of potatoes on the farm. There was no payment involved, but they helped with the labour – spreading the manure, planting, and, in the Autumn, picking the potatoes. In fact, it had been a tradition for generations for different farms to be paired with different cottages. It was a symbiotic relationship – borne of the farmer's and the cottager's need for each other (a cottage was a dwelling with very little land, or none at all). Very often the breadwinner from the cottage would go off to seek employment in the coal mines of South Wales, or maybe in the woollen mills which were very numerous in the lower reaches of the parish of Llangeler.

During the manuring of the potato fields, the horse would be driven through the rows so that the wheels of the cart would fit into the two outer rows. The manure would be ejected in heaps seven yards apart. When the field happened to be far from the yard, at the high end of the farm, two horses were employed to pull the cart – one horse in the shafts and one in front, called a tracing horse (*'ceffyl traso'*) – see the following photograph. When a horse pulled a cart on the flat, he would go at quite a leisurely pace, but uphill he would go faster because the faster he went, the sooner he would reach the top.

Perfect team work

(The Eric Guy Collection, MERL, University of Reading)

The day of planting the potatoes, the manure had to be spread the same day in case the manure would dry out too much if left too long. The seed potatoes would have been bagged up ready – probably on a wet day when we couldn't work on the land. Over winter these were buried in case of frost. On the day of planting, a big sack (the '*llywionen*') was worn, tied around the waist to act as a large pouch to carry the potatoes during the planting. It was hard work, but very enjoyable, and everyone smelled of manure! Some of the old people used to say 'plenty of manure is a sure sign of future wealth'.

As soon as the planting was finished, the rows were closed in again using a horse and ridger. I think that opening and closing the rows was one of the most skilful jobs to be had on the farm, because the horses had to be driven in a straight line, the ridges had to be held and kept to the same depth, and the headland had to be left for seven yards – the same as for ploughing.

Our next task after doing the potatoes was sowing the mangolds – which were sown on top of the ridges after the rows had been closed.

See page 136

Notice the horse in the background pulling the drill to sow the root crops
– e.g. sweeds and mangolds

(Farmer and Stockbreeder, MERL, University of Reading)

The mangolds were drilled or sown using a one-row drill which was pulled by one horse. 'Red intermediate' and 'yellow globe' were the two most popular breeds of mangolds. Kale was also sown the same time as the mangolds, and the two most popular breeds were 'thousand headed' and 'narrow stem'.

Swedes

Sweeds were always sown as near as possible to the 3rd of June. The breed that suited us best was 'Tiperary'.

As soon as the barley was sown, the grass seeds were sown on the same field – what is known as undersowing. The most popular breed of barley was '*Yr Hen Gymro*' (The Old Welshman), but, alas, it is unavailable now.

Here, I should mention that in any Spring, convoys of horses and carts would make the annual trip to the lime kilns, the other side of Carmarthen to Llangendeirn and Llandybie. This was, of course, before the advent of trains and lorries. It was quite common to see a convoy of over fifty horses going through Carmarthen. I quote from D. Parry Jones (1948, p.99):

> *Carmarthen town in its long history must have been roused from its sleep more than once by the sound of horses' hooves, and many echoes must have been awakened as these carts rumbled over its narrow cobbled streets accompanied by the shouts of the drivers, the clanging of the heavy chain traces, the tramp of the hooves, and equally heavy tramp of hobnailed boots. These noises have*

long died away, and nothing can again disturb their echoes. The journey home was more leisurely, and at 'The Rock and Fountain Inn', the home side of Carmarthen, man and beast stopped for a well earned rest.

The tramping noise of the hobnailed boots was exacerbated by the fact that tracing horses had to be run through town.

But I divert – back to the farm tasks. The barley field to be reseeded had to be limed. Any farmyard manure that was left at the end of the winter was taken out on to the hayfields in heaps and spread. When the hay was subsequently cut, it was easy to see where the heaps had been, by the difference in the lushness of the crop.

By about the middle or the end of April, the cattle – who had been in since the autumn – were ready to go out. They seemed to know this from the lengthening the days and the shortening of the nights.

There were signs all around that the summer was coming. We would notice the geese eating the lime off the whitewashed farm walls, in order to get calcium for their eggshells, and we'd notice them picking up bits of straw in their bills and carrying it away to make nests. There were other signs – such as the gorse and blackthorn coming into bloom. It was time to turn out the young cattle, and they used to be driven up to the moor and our top fields. That seemed to be a very long journey to me when I was young. All hands were needed for this task because the young cattle, when they had cooled down from their taste of freedom (which involved galloping to and fro, kicking their heels in the air, and sometimes picking a fight with each other) would start to feel homesick and try to retrace their steps and go back towards the farmstead. It was as much as we could all do – plus two or three dogs –to stop them from going back. It only goes to show that cattle feel safe when near home – just like everyone else.

A few days later the milking cows would be turned out. By this time the mangolds would have finished. They were a very important ingredient in the milking cows' diet in the early days of milk production. Twice a day we would turn the handle of the pulper until the big tub was full of chipped mangolds. Sometimes I would try one for myself – it tasted so sweet, like a salad ingredient you would find in the Mediterranean. A bowlful of pulped mangolds and another of crushed oats twice a day, each with a little boiled barley added was a most important feed. A small amount of bought concentrated feed was used as well, but the emphasis was on home-grown organic food.

When the milking cows were turned out, they always grazed the bottom fields nearest the farmstead, as they had to be fetched in for milking twice a day, and it was obviously a shorter distance and more convenient.

After turning out the cattle, one of the next tasks was to spring clean the cowshed. This involved scrubbing the stalls, brushing off all the cobwebs, and whitewashing the walls. When the weather was favourable, all the farm buildings would be whitewashed on the outside as well. This was done again in the autumn, before the weather turned. By this time, the hay fields would have been chain harrowed and rolled, ready to be kept for hay.

A common Spring time scene

The Spring work by this time had all been accomplished so that
nature could take its course. Here I want to include a practice that
took place every year on June 24th ('*Dydd Gwyl Ifan*', which is St
John the Baptist's day) and that is the fair held at
Bwlchyddwyrhos. It was known locally as '*Ffair Gooseberries*',
and people came from near and far to join in the games. The main

game was '*cnapan*' – similar to hockey. There was also weight lifting and tug-of-war. I also remember my mother mentioning *Ffair New Inn* in the parish of Penbryn, Cardiganshire, where she grew up. These fairs had their origins somewhere in the dim and distant past, but have all now disappeared.

CHAPTER 12

Summer

Everyone looked forward to summer. At the end of May, in the potato fields the potatoes and mangolds had started to grow, and needed weeding and hoeing. For this we used the scuffler. This was similar to a horse plough, but instead of the moulder it had one wheel in the middle at the front followed by five blades that opened up the ground in between the rows, digging it and leaving the weeds on the surface to wilt. It was drawn by one horse walking between the rows. In a couple of days the potatoes were hoed, then scuffled again before being earthed up again by using the 'double tom' or ridger. Next the mangolds would have the same treatment, except they were singled instead of being earthed up. The same would apply to the kale and the sweeds later on. What with one thing and another, the potato fields took up a lot of time during the summer. The hoeing and the singling both constituted slow and careful work, and we took a lot of pride in these tasks.

Towards the end of June, all the sheep would have to be gathered and taken to be washed. Not every farm had a good water supply for this purpose, and sheep would have to be walked to a communal washing pool.

A typical communal washing pool

Here the river would be damned. There was such a place in
Cenarth on the river Teifi, where the coracle men would be on
hand to assist. Two or three days later, the shearing would take
place. I remember the old hand shears *'gwellau'*, before the advent
of the mechanical shears.

Before the end of the summer, the sheep would have to be dipped
to prevent 'maggoting'. Only some farms in the locality were
equipped with a sheep dip. Everyone around here went to 'Trial
Mawr' farm to dip their sheep. In those days, the local policeman
would have to be present to supervise the dipping.

But it was haymaking that took up most of the summer, especially
if the weather was unfavourable. Over my lifetime, I have
experienced at first hand the changes which have taken place -
from hay being turned by hand rakes and pitched by pitchers, to
small bales, then to large round bales, and now big square bales
weighing nearly a ton and handled by tractors. We don't have to
look too far back to a time when there was no mechanism of any
kind involved in haymaking. The only tool was the sickle until the
12th century, when the scythe was introduced, a wooden rake, and

a pitchfork (*'picwarch'*). There were no other tools involved apart from an ox and cart.

The scythe was first used by the Scythians, a nomadic people who, about 600 BC, were located in Armenia and around Lake Urmia. They grew hemp and harvested it with a hand reaper which we call a scythe. They also grew cannabis which they used to inhale during funeral rituals. The scythe probably arrived in Britain some time during the Dark Ages, and remained the main mowing implement until mechanisation took place.

Scything or mowing was done very early in the morning when the grass was covered in dew, as it was more difficult to cut when it was dry. Then the hay cut on the previous days could be turned, or carted it in – whichever was appropriate.

It was around 1900 that the horse-drawn mower became quite common. It was pulled by two horses with a long shaft between them (*'y powlen'*) which controlled the height of the cutting bar. The pulling was effected by the *'cambren'*. The farmer would sit on the seat of the mower to drive, and control the horses and lifting the cutting bar at the corners of the field.

A typical haymaking scene

Soon after the mower was invented, the swath turner (*'trowr yr ystod'*), the hay rake, and the side rake were developed and these became very popular. These three machines were pulled by one horse, driven by the farmer from the seat of the machine. The side rake took over from the hay rake because it could be adjusted to row up the hay – something which was done up until then by using the big rake, and before that, the tumbler. By the way, the Welsh name for a row of hay was a *'carfan'*.

The next invention was the hayloader. The two types that are familiar to me are the McCormick International (which was made

in Chicago, USA) and the Bamford (made in Utoxeter). Nicolson
Albion Denning of Chard was another maker of farm machinery
that was very common. The hayloader fitted behind the gambo,
and the gambo was pulled by the horse so that the wheels were on
both sides of the row in order that the hayloader could lift the hay
as it went over it. There were usually one or two men on the
gambo stacking the hay.

All the hay was then carted to the rick-yard (*'yr ydlan'*) where it
would be built up into a haystack or ricks. The haystack was
always round, whereas the rick was rectangular. After they were
built, they were raked down and plucked before they were
thatched.

After the First World War, the Dutch barns started to appear, and
became a common feature of every farm. With them came an
excellent feat of engineering – the pitcher (*'y pitshwr'*). Within
this locality, they were made by Jones, Lion, Cardigan. This
pitcher could lift half a gambo of hay in one go and transport it
back to anywhere in the shed by means of hooks, pulleys, and
ropes powered by one horse. One of the first jobs I remember
doing regarding haymaking was leading the horse in the pitcher.

Those days are almost forgotten now, disappeared into the mists of time, but I remember there being part of a close knit community where every farmer and cottager helped one another. Everybody was looked after by the neighbours – nobody was left out. The farmer planned mowing time so that it didn't clash with the bringing in of the neighbour's hay. The same thoughtfulness extended to the smallholders who didn't have their own implements, so that their harvest would also be safely gathered in. After all, everyone depended on everyone else. As well as the haymaking, the other farm work had to be done – for instance, the milking and taking the milk out to the milkstand. In our case, the milkstand was exactly a mile from the farm, at the junction of our road with the Bancyffordd road.

The milk lorries, who used to collect the milk from the milk stands
delivering to the depot at Newcastle Emlyn
(Photograph by kind permission of Ken Jones, Bryn Haul, Newcastle Emlyn)

On the very spot where our milkstand stood, there is now a

bungalow and a blacksmith shop. Today's blacksmith's is no

longer like the old one I remember from my youth where the

blacksmith (*'y gof'*) would stand between the fire and the anvil (*'yr*

eingon'), the metal, red hot, held by a tong in his left hand, and a

hammer in his right. It was quite common on a wet day to see four

or five horses queuing up to be shod. All the horseshoes were

made on the spot and burned on to the hoof before nailing.

The local carpenter and the blacksmith would keep one day of the week free so that they could get together to fit the steel bands on the cartwheels. The cartwheel was made by the local carpenter ('*saer*') who used well seasoned elm for the hub, the spokes were of oak, and the rim made from ash, or sometimes elm. The blacksmith made the steel band slightly smaller than the diameter of the wheel. When the carpenter and blacksmith got together to fit the steel, the blacksmith would put the steel band into his fire until it was red hot. The steel expanded so that it could be fitted on to the wheel with tongs. Then it could be hammered into place and a large amount of water poured on to the wheel all around, to prevent the wood from catching fire. The carpenter, blacksmith, and a couple more people would all pour the water at the same time. As the metal band cooled, it contracted to fit tightly over the wood. You could hear the cracking as the whole assembly was bound together to give a lifetime of trouble free service.

Fixing the steel band

(Farmers' Weekly, MERL, University of Reading)

The carpenter was the ladder maker, the gate maker, and the wooden rake maker, so, whatever the weather was, the carpenter could always find something to do. To make his ladders he used well seasoned birch, with oak rungs. It was very common for the farmer to fell a tree and take it to the carpenter to be sawn up and made into gates. Every carpenter had his own pattern when it came to making gates.

Because the only means of transport was by riding on horseback or being pulled by a horse drawn vehicle, the saddler was another person very much in demand. Because every item of the harness was leather (apart from the brasses and buckles), repairs or replacements was the affair of the saddler. Incidentally, four of my father's brothers became saddlers.

The mason also was as much in demand as the other craftsmen. Building a house out of stone quarried locally must have been a very satisfying achievement. Look around this area alone, and see the houses, stables and barns still standing, proud and a little sad to see what has happened around them.

After the hay harvest, there was spare time to single the sweeds, [swedes] and also cut the thistles in the grazing and corn fields should there be any in them. A scythe ('*y bladur*') was used for this purpose in the grazing fields, but in the corn fields a different method was employed. In one hand a stick was held with a blade attached at right angles to the stick. In the other hand was held a long stick with a fork at the end. The thistle would be held firm with the fork, so that it could be cut with the blade, and left there. Using this method, and by walking carefully, the thistles were controlled without disturbing the corn too much, and without bending or kneeling down. 'Trashing' (cutting back) the lane and opening ditches was another job that was done. In fact, while the fine weather lasted and the days were long, we would get as many tasks done as possible before the autumn.

The Corn Harvest

By the middle of August the corn would be almost ripe enough to cut. The first field to ripen was the field of black oats. Two well know breeds were '*ceirch tŷ bach*' and '*ceirch du*', '*ceirch*' being the Welsh word for oats. The black oats needed to be cut before fully ripe, for if left to ripen too much, the heads would come off, and all that would be harvested would be straw. It was cut when it was 'the colour of a pigeon' ('*lliw'r scythan*').

The last field to be harvested was usually the barley field – all the fields were cut in the order in which they were ripening.

The earliest tool to be used to cut the corn was the sickle (*cryman*). It had been used long before the Romans came to this country, but by the 16th century it had been replaced by the scythe – which had only previously been used for cutting grass or hay.

When the corn was cut by a row of men, the women and children would follow and gather the corn into bundles, then bind it with a short rope which they made on the spot out of loose straw. The little rope is termed a '*rheffyn*', and the bound bundle of straw or sheaf, an '*ysgub*'.

Towards the end of the 1800's a new machine – the reaper – was beginning to appear on some farms. It had a cutting bar working from a chain powered by the main wheel – similar to a binder or mower – i.e. a 'ground drive' (when the wheel stopped, the cutting stopped, unlike the engine driven machine). The reaper cut the corn, and threw it behind it in bundles, ready to be tied. Before the reaper was popular, some of the hay mowers were fitted with two seats, one for the driver who drove the horses and one for a person sitting on his right-hand side to use the rake. The corn was raked back in bundles, ready to be tied by someone following the mower. This was called 'raking out' or '*crafu mâs*'. According to Everyman's Encyclopaedia (1978, Vol. 10, p. 238), the reaper was first designed by the Rev. Patrick Bell, around 1826.

'Crafu mâs'

(TheArwyn Wi lliams collection, Clwb Hanes Llanfihangel-ar-Arth History Club)

It was round about the beginning of the 1900's and when the knotter was invented, that the binder first appeared. My grandfather had the first binder in our area in 1908. It was a McCormick International right-hand cut. These machines were made with the cutting bar either on the right hand side or the left. It was pulled like the reaper by either two or three horses depending on the field. The edges of the field had been previously cut by scythe, and the cut corn tied in the old-fashioned way. This was to make room for the horses and binder, so that the corn didn't get trampled.

After the corn was cut, the sheaves were stacked up in fours. The corn stook was known as a '*stacon*', and left for about ten days. These were checked daily in case some had fallen with the wind or crows had pulled them down – those that were affected were made good. After about ten days, the sheaves were stacked up into little field stacks containing about fourteen stooks (or fifty sheaves, or thereabouts). In some parts of Wales these were individually called '*shogwrn*', and in other parts '*sopin*'.

One stack would be commenced with one stook, then other sheaves stacked around the stook until a point was reached where only the top of the last four sheaves were exposed at the top. Every sheaf was almost upright, so that the rain was thrown off. I have seen some fields filled with stacks of corn left out until nearly Christmas, because of the severity of the weather, and only the top four sheaves were wasted – even these could be fed to the dry cows.

When I was young it used to be the practice that when a farmer retired he would hold a corn sale as soon as he completed his corn harvest. The reason for this was that the purchaser could move the corn stacks directly from the corn field to his own farm. Quite often some of them were bought by the new occupier moving in. For him, the corn stacks were on his new farm already. The main sale of the livestock would be held about October time when everything else was sold under the hammer - the implements, tools, and everything else. It took the farmer nearly a lifetime to collect all his tools, horses, cows and pigs, and in half a day, they were scattered to the four corners of the county, as well as locally of course. It was the custom not to sell the hay, but to offer it under valuation to the new tenant or owner – which was really very sensible, not to need to move loads of loose hay through country lanes.

But to return to the corn harvest. The next stage was carting in. First the field stacks were opened, and the sheaves put upright in twos leaning on each other so that the wind blew between them. The few sheaves that had been next to the ground at the base of the stack were also shaken, and laid so that the part that had been next to the ground was exposed to the wind. These were then left to dry for a few hours until, when shaken, they made a noise like the wind rustling through the trees ('*rwshan*').

Next the gambo was loaded with the sheaves. We could get quite a lot on the gambo because sheaves were a lot easier to stack than loose hay. Then the load was taken down to the stack yard where big round stacks would be built. The round stack was called the '*helem*'.

There was one man on the '*helem*'. He would work around, kneeling on each sheaf as he placed it as he went along, making sure that the middle was much higher that the edge to make sure that no water could seep in. Throwing the sheaves from the gambo was quite a skill. You were expected to throw the sheaf so that it turned in the air before finally landing conveniently in front of the man kneeling on the stacks. It took some getting used to, but once mastered it was very pleasant and rewarding work. As well as round stacks, sheaves would sometimes be made into rectangular stacks, or ricks.

Many years ago, as soon as the corn fields were cleared, people were allowed to come and glean ('*lloffa'*) the fields for bits of corn and straw (*'llofion'*) that were going to waste, and they took the bundles home with them. When that tradition died out, farmers had wooden 'stubble rakes' (*'raca safol'*) made by the local carpenter. The stubble rake was about four or five feet wide with two handles to it so that it could be pulled along until it had enough straw to make a sheaf. Then the rake would be lifted and the process repeated. Another person following would bind the corn into a sheaf. I remember my father using a stubble rake. The rake was half carried and half pulled so that the impression one got was that the task was not very difficult – but the likelihood is that this was only due to the skilful way that father was handling the rake.

In the early 19th century, it was the custom or tradition in Cardiganshire, at the end of the summer, for young men to go with their scythes to cut in the cornfields of Herefordshire or Gloucestershire. They would be away from home for about six weeks, moving from one farm to another in gangs. Today, it's not a row of men with their scythes that can be seen, but a row of combine harvesters moving slowly across the fields like some giant monsters covered in clouds of dust.

CHAPTER 13
Autumn

Autumn, when I was young, was one of the most pleasant of all the seasons. Everything seemed quiet. You could hear someone whistling over half a mile away through the early morning mist. The swallows were congregating in rows on the cowshed roof (the cowshed had been their home all summer) ready to fly away for the winter. The hedgerows were heavy with their different coloured berries, and the leaves were changing colour and acquiring rich autumn hues.

After the corn had all been carted in, the stacks and ricks that were to be kept over winter would have to be thatched. This was a very skilled craft that every farmer mastered. In this area, straw was the most popular thatch, but some farmers used rushes if they happened to have plenty of the plants on their farm.

Thatching the '*helmi*' (round stacks)

(The Eric Guy collection, MERL, University of Reading)

Threshing days

There would be one day of threshing in the Autumn, and another in
the Spring – about March. During the Autumnal threshing, some
of the straw would be put aside ready for thatching. First the straw
was taken in bundles and pulled by both ends several times so that
the straw fibres were long and parallel before putting in large
bundles or trusses ready to be taken up on to the stack. It was
time-consuming work, but very satisfying.

Until the time of World War 1 and afterwards in some parts, threshing took place in the barn using a stationary thresher powered by a water wheel. The weight of water filling up the spoons of the water wheel caused the mill wheel to turn. From the centre of the wheel came a shaft (*warthid*) which turned a pulley in the barn. The latter turned a drive belt connected to the pulley on the thrasher, winnowing machine, grinding mill, or whatever needed to be turned.

If there was no stream available to create a mill pond, a *partmâs* was used. The *partmâs* had a gear box connected to a shaft, as with the water wheel, but this time powered by a horse walking in circles. The shaft was connected to a pulley in the barn.

The first threshing machine with a drum as we know it was invented by Andrew Meikel in 1786. Prior to that, the corn was hammered with two pieces of wood (fists) each having a triangular flat beating end, hinged to the shaft by a piece of leather, to separate the grain from the straw. Conditions were very dusty during threshing in the barn, so some form of ventilation was needed. This explains why every one of the old barns had a front and back door opposite to each other to crate a though draught to get rid of the dust.

I'll return to my memories of threshing days. All the neighbours would come and help, because it was a communal operation. The threshing machine would move from farm to farm, and usually stayed on each farm for one day.

The first task was to set the thresher. This involved making it level, either by putting a plank under the wheels on one side or digging under the wheels on the other side. Blocks were utilised to stop it moving with the vibration during the threshing operation. By this time, men were arriving from neighbouring farms (in those days there were at least two or three men on every farm). During threshing, there were always two men on the thresher itself, two throwing the sheaves on to the thresher, two pitching the straw on to the straw rick, one man on the straw rick itself, one man in charge of the corn sacks, and at least two or three men carrying the sacks filled with corn, which had to be thrown on to their backs.

At mid-day, the machine was stopped, and everyone would come into the house for a roast dinner. Two tables were put together for this purpose, so that everyone could eat together.

Just after the Second World War, two Polish men came to farm Bwlchclawdd Morgan – a local farm. They were a Mr. Filipek and a Mr Paryż, two very nice, well mannered gentlemen. They, like all the neighbours, would come to help on threshing day. When all the men came into the house at dinner time, everyone would take off their caps, sit down, and start to eat. But not Mr Paryż. He turned to mother and asked her whether he could help her in any way. Mother would reply, 'No thank you. I'm tending on you, because you came to help us with the threshing'. She remarked privately later that that was the first time anyone had asked whether they could they help her. The two Polish men farmed for many years, and were good neighbours, good farmers, and good friends.

About 1952, the big stationery baler was invented so that the straw could be baled as soon as it came out of the thresher. It was made by Denning of Chard, and did away with the need for the straw rick.

The following day, we all met up again on another farm to do the same thing all over again.

Potato picking

Potato picking was similar to threshing in that it was a communal activity, and we had a field full of helpers.

Some time at the beginning of the 20th century, a potato digger was invented. It had a blade on it that went under the potato row. Above that was a wheel with tines on it to throw the potatoes sideways as it was pulled along, making it easy for the people to pick them into wooden baskets (*'wintelli'*) made by the local basket makers. These baskets were very lightweight and easy to handle. For example, when they were thrown forwards during picking they always landed the right way up. Their frame was from hazel and the basket from plaited willow. They were very strong, and lasted for many years. The families who were allowed to plant a couple of rows in the field always came to help with the potato picking, and at the end of the day would be given the loan of a horse and cart to take their potatoes home. The scene of about seven or eight horses and carts standing patiently in a row on the field was an unforgettable sight. Carts were tub carts so that they could tip their loads. When the first cart was fully loaded the order was given for the owner to take the cart to the farmstead where the potatoes were stored. This was usually a shed with a wide door so that the cart could be reversed in. The horse not only had to pull the cart but was also trained to reverse it. It was up to the skill of the driver to make sure that the hub of the cartwheel did not hit the post or the wall. If it did, it was called '*bwlo*', because the Welsh word for a hub is a '*bwlin*'. There were always one or two men in charge of the stock of potatoes to make sure that they were tipped properly, and also to make sure that there was plenty of straw beween the potatoes and the wall to protect them from frost. Some farms preferred to store potatoes and other root crops in clamps outside. These were protected by covering them with earth and straw. In Welsh they were called '*y cladd*' – a burial.

As soon as the first cart had been unloaded, the horse and the empty cart were taken back to the field for refilling, on the way passing another laden cart. And that was the scene all day – people in the field picking and loading, and the horses transporting the potatoes to the farmstead.

Food was taken out to the field at midday, unlike the custom on threshing day. Everyone sat in a row by the hedge to eat. The following day, the whole procedure was repeated on another farm. When the day was over and everyone was making for home, the most common phrase was 'See you tomorrow', and I wonder whether the horses too said the same to each other.

Getting the potatoes in was only the beginning, because later in the winter they needed to be sorted. The seed potatoes would be picked out, the small and rubbishy ones would be given to the pigs, and the good ones weighed, put into 1 cwt. sacks, and the sacks sewn (not tied) before being taken to the potato merchant (Mr. Davies, of Jones and Davies, Llandysul). Mr. Davies had trucks on the sidings at Llandysul railway station, and we loaded the sacks of potatoes on these to be taken away to Swansea and Cardiff.

But back to the harvest. As soon as every farm had their potatoes in, the next job was the mangolds before the frost set in. It was one of the coldest jobs, even when it wasn't freezing. For this, we each had a big knife. The mangold would be pulled out of the ground by the leaves, roughly cleaned of earth using the back of the knife, and with a single movement the leaves cut off and the mangold thrown skilfully onto a pile between the second and third rows. The reason for the position of the pile of mangolds was that we pulled two rows at a time so that the cart or trailer had enough room to go between the rows to collect the piles. When all the mangolds had been pulled, there was a mound of mangold leaves and a mound of mangolds alternating over the field.

We used the same method for the sweeds sometime before Christmas.

October was the time of the year when most of the farm sales took place. When a farmer retired, if there was no-one in the family to take over the farm, a new family would be introduced to the neighbourhood and soon fitted in with the local ways. Farm sales (auctions) were again dependent on the good will of neighbours who came to help prepare for sale day. All the machinery would be washed, cleaned thoroughly, and sometimes painted. Particular attention was given to the harness, which was subsequently hung up on a frame made by the local carpenter a few days earlier. It was usually placed near the gateway of the field nearest the homestead, where the machinery was also lined up ready to be sold. All the tools and small things that had accumulated over the years had to be cleaned and put together in the barn to be sold at the end of auction day.

The day started very early. All the neighbours came to help gather the stock in. The milking cows were the first to be tied up, washed and brushed. These were followed by the horses, who were brushed until they were shining. Next it was the turn of the sheep and the young cattle, who were normally in the furthest field from the house.

Everything had to look its best before the people started to arrive. After all, when a farmer and his wife have spent a lifetime caring for their farm and stock, as well as observing every duty and custom of good neighbourliness, they could take pride in the fact that they had done their best, and for a very long time their neighbours remembered it.

Fairs were very important in those days. It was at the cattle and horse fairs where the stock would be bought and sold by the drovers.

They took them to England to sell until the railways came. Then they were transported by rail, and the cattle markets opened near the station where the cattle could be loaded as soon as they were sold. We still have the fun fairs for entertainment purposes, but it seems to have been forgotten that these fun fairs are held on the same days as the old cattle fairs were held.

One of the most important fairs in this area was the Carmarthen fair which was held on the 14th November every year. It was called '*Ffair glyngaeaf*', and it was the custom for the farm servant ('*gwas*') to be given a week's holiday from the 7th to the 14th of November. It was the Carmarthen fair that was the start and end of a farm servant's year.

If a farm servant wanted to end his contract with the farmer, he had to give plenty of notice in order to give sufficient time to find his replacement. On some of the bigger farms, two or three servants would be employed, and plenty of notice was important if more than one wanted to leave. One custom regarding farm servants was that if a servant remained on the same farm for seven years he was given a heifer, whereas a maid servant, if she stayed for six years, was given a pair of blankets. Where there were two or three servants on a farm, the youngest would be called '*y gwas bach*' and the eldest '*y gwas mawr*' – the little servant and the big servant respectively. It was part of the hierarchy. Fifty years ago, within an area of about a square mile from our farm, I remember about twenty farm servants working on adjacent farms. Today there are none. The days when the cottagers and farmers were interdependent have passed - perhaps due to the total efficiency and mechanical power of modern farm machinery. Gone therefore is the harvest crowd that filled the field with happiness, and these bonds that held the rural structure together have been broken.

In fairness to the loyal and hard working farm servants, it was simple economic factors that tipped the scale, making people realise that there was a prospect of a better life and more money in engineering or on a building site – very much as the coal mines of South Wales a hundred years ago that were the attraction.

CHAPTER 14
Winter

After the Carmarthen fair, it was time to get the cattle in for the winter. All the young stock had to be fetched down from the top fields to join the rest of the stock inside until the Spring. The cows were let out to have water twice a day – every day, seven days a week all through the winter. The rest of the time, they were tied to the stall – which was wooden in those days. Bolted onto the stall was a slider about three feet long so as to be long enough for the cow to lie down. On the slider was a steel ring with a turner on it ('*y troiwr*') so that if the cow turned around, she wouldn't choke. The cow tie ('*yr eirw*') – worn round the neck of the cow - fitted on to a ring next to the turner, and directly in front of the cow was the manger for feeding the mangolds, oats, hay, and anything else the cow had.

In front of the row of cows was the '*wâc*' – the feeding walk – separated from the mangers by a wooden partition, about four feet high, the '*côr*'. Over that we fed the hay. There was a door from the 'wâc' out to the hayshed. Behind the row of cows in the stalls there was a step down of about 5″, and behind that was an area we called 'y sodren', which would be cleaned out by wheelbarrow into the dung heap or 'domen'. Every farm worker took a certain amount of pride in his dung heap. There would be a long plank of wood, 6 - 7″ wide, by about 3 - 4″ thick, and anything up to 20′ long, against the heap. We pushed the wheelbarrow up a slope to the top of the dung heap to empty it. By doing that, it took less space and looked much tidier.

The stable was similar in construction to the cowshed, except it had no step - thus the 'sodren' was all level. There was also no feeding walk because the horses were fed from the loft above the stable into a feeding rack or 'rhostal'. As with the cowshed, the stable was cleaned out two or three times a day by wheelbarrow.

Towards the middle of February, one of the topics of conversation amongst the farmers was 'yr ogor' – how much animal feed they had left over. The old people used to say that half a bay of hay left over from the winter months was better than money in the bank. There used to be a poem that everyone knew:

Haner y llafur Gŵyl Fair, a haner y gwair Gŵyl Dewi
(Half the corn should be used by St Mary's Day, and half by St
David's Day – which, incidentally, were Feb 12th and March 1st
respectively).

Gŵyl Fair y Canwyllau is the feast of the Purification of the Virgin
Mary. It is halfway through the winter – which starts about the
middle of November, and lasts until the 10th of May – from *Calan
Gaeaf* until *Calan Mai*. (On this day, also, the geese and ducks
start to lay). Some people think that this is the source of St
Valentine's Day – in Welsh, *Gwyl y Cariadon.*

The process of feeding cattle loose hay in those days was quite
laborious. First we cut a square area – about 4' by 4' at the top of
the hayshed with a hay knife. This is a long blade with a handle
across the top. The hay was cut the length of the knife and was
thrown down. Then the process repeated every day until the floor
was reached. Then we would start again at the top. The wedge of
hay that was cut was called the '*wanaf*'. A two pronged pitchfork
('*picwarch*') was used to carry the hay into the feeding walk, but to
carry hay some distance a '*llywanen*' was used. This was a very
big bran sack, which was opened up into a square with a knot that

Compare with p 96

136

would be tied in two opposite corners. A short piece of line was tied to the knot, the '*llywanen*' laid down flat, and the hay piled on to it. When there was enough hay, two opposite corners were grasped, the hay and the '*llywanen*' heaved on to one's back, and the hay could be carried wherever needed.

Not only the milking cows would need to be let out for water twice a day - it was the same for the horses, unless they were used for something - which very often happened - such as carting the muck out, pulling trees, or fetching something. Between feeding and looking after all the cattle and horses, quite a lot of the day was taken up.

Sometime around the beginning of December, it was time to kill the first pig. Usually one was killed well before Christmas, and one in the New Year. This was in order to have time to salt and cure the first one before starting on the second, at a time of no electricity, and hence no fridges and freezers.

After killing the pig it would be hung in the barn for 24 hours, then taken down and cut up. The hams, gammons, and sides were taken into the dairy and laid on the slate slabs to be salted. I well remember the big blocks of salt I had to slice with a big knife and then rolled with a bottle until it was fine and loose, to rub into the meat. Everything else was made into faggots and brawn. There would be some fresh unsalted meat left over, such as the fry, ribs, etc. This meat was shared with neighbours while it was fresh – there being no such things as 'fridges in those days, and the favour would be returned when they, in turn, killed their pigs.

It was not only the farms where the pig was killed. Every house and cottage had a pig sty ('*twlc*') where the owners fattened a pig or two every year. The pig sty wasn't very far from the house. Indeed, in some of the cottages it was actually attached to the house so that it was near enough to take to it something like potato peelings, or anything from the garden that was going to waste. It was recycling at its best. At this time of the year – after 21st December, the shortest day, everyone talked about the days getting longer: '*Cam ceiliog cyn Calan, awr gyfan Hen Galan*' (One cockerel's step before New Year's Day, and a whole hour before *Calan Hên*' – which is on the 12th January).

Christmas time

Christmas Day when I was young, according to my understanding, hadn't changed at all from the time that my parents were young. I will recount what I remember.

The first sign that Christmas was on its way was when Miss Evans, the infants' teacher, put up the Christmas decorations in the classroom. She put an eighteen inch Father Christmas on the window sill, and warned us all that he (the Father Christmas) was watching, and that he had a long memory!

The second clue was when Mother mixed the plum pudding in a big earthenware bowl. The bowl was so big and heavy that it was as much as anyone could do to lift it onto the table. Mother mixed enough pudding to fill twelve basins, and that evening, Father covered and tied them ready to be boiled the following day. This was done in a big cast iron boiler, big enough to hold the twelve basins. The smell filled up the whole house. The first pudding was eaten on feathering day, the second on Christmas Day, the third on New Year's Day, and the rest every Sunday until they were gone.

Exactly a week before Christmas Day, the geese and turkeys were feathered. It was a long day starting very early and finishing late, but feathering was always completed in one day. The same people came to help every year – they had been coming from before my time. The geese took the longest to feather because of their fine down which had to be pinched, not plucked like the turkeys. In those days, pillows and cushions were filled with feathers, and mattresses were filled with straw. Big flour sacks were filled with the feathers by the children – a task given to them to keep them occupied. Mother was in charge of dressing the fowls, and by the end of the day the slate slabs in the dairy were full of dressed poultry.

Incidentally, unlike the turkeys, the geese had a lot of fat. Goose grease was always in demand as a remedy for several ailments. If anyone strained a muscle or joint, they would rub in goose grease (*'sâm gwyddau'*), and if a cow had a hard udder, warm goose grease was the remedy. If you had to use it on your leg for some reason or other, one thing was certain, the dogs would follow you everywhere because they loved the smell of the goose grease!

But back to the Christmas poultry. The following day people came to collect the poultry that they had ordered. The same customers came every year, and the order would go from one year to the next.

Quite a number of the poultry went as far as the Rhondda and Cardiff, and these poultry had to be packed in individual boxes and sealed. I can well remember the boxes being tied and a candle being used to melt the sealing wax over the knots. The hot wax would drip onto the knots, so that when the boxes arrived at their destination, the recipient knew the box had not been tampered with because of the unbroken seals. The only way these poultry could travel was by train, and I remember going with my father to Llandysul railway station to send them off. My father would also send a telegram to the various customers saying when the trains were due to arrive.

The farm was a lot quieter for the next couple of days after feathering, and we had to get used to it. The only geese that were left were only the breeding geese and the gander for the following year.

One of the nicest memories I have is of going round the cattle and horses on Christmas Eve to give them their last meal for the day and make sure that they were safe for the night. I remember coming through the cowshed, when Father said 'Can you see them kneeling by the manger?' 'Yes' I said. 'That's how they kept the Baby Jesus warm on that first Christmas. Because of that, their breath always smells sweet'.

Christmas Day always started an hour earlier than usual, because the milk lorry driver always left a note saying he would be an hour earlier on the two days – Christmas Day and Boxing Day. Cows had to be milked, and also had to be fed and watered together with the young stock and horses. Also stables and cowsheds had to be cleaned out. The pony was harnessed and got ready to pull the milk cart containing the milk churns to the milk stand, exactly a mile from our farm. The pony was the only horse to work on Christmas Day, and as soon as he was back from taking the milk out, he was put back in the stable.

Until about 10 o'clock, Christmas day was very much like any other day, except that Father Christmas had been leaving presents, and Mother had decorated every window with holly – which was the only decoration. We never had a Christmas tree or fairy lights – well, anyway, there was no electricity anywhere in this area until 1963.

After all the work was done, Father and one or two of us went to the church for the Christmas service. On our return, Mother had the dinner almost ready – it was goose of course, followed by plum pudding.

I am almost sure that every Christmas Day had probably been much the same for over a hundred years – apart from the fact that we had a wind-up gramophone, which we used every Christmas afternoon, listening to songs sung by David Lloyd, Madam Adelina Patti, and Gracie Fields.

When Father was young, Boxing Day and New Year's Day were holidays. There would be sports – racing and jumping - in one of the fields belonging to The Lamb Inn. All the young people would congregate and compete in a friendly way. On New Year's Day, it was the tradition for children to go from door to door, singing for '*calenig*' – sweets or money.

143

As soon as Christmas was over, everyone looked forward to the days getting longer – this was especially true of the farming community. They remarked on the day lengthening by 'the step of a cockerel' on New Year's Day, but by a whole hour by old 'Calan' (the old New Year's Day which is on 12th January). Old 'Calan', when it was celebrated at Llandysul Church, involved representatives of every church in the group of local churches taking it in turns to recite from the Scriptures and sing an anthem. This custom originated nearly two hundred years ago to replace a previous custom, which was a very rowdy rough undisciplined football match between two parishes. The goalposts were the door frames of the respective parish churches. Probably this custom derived from a more primitive time when there was a state of hostility between the two parishes. The football match always ended in fights when several people had limbs broken accompanied by lots of animosity and ill feeling.

By the time *Calan Hên* had passed and the days were lengthening, the farm work of feeding and looking after the stock carried on as usual, as well as hedging *('cloddio)'* – which meant repairing or rebuilding hedges damaged by stock or rabbits, which were plentiful. Hedge laying was another winter task, when the growth

Llandysul and Llanwenog

was skilfully laid. Thorn hedges were the best to lay, where every little gap could be filled and made stock proof. We, as children, were always being warned of the dangers of blackthorn and whitethorn poisoning. The hawthorn was especially dangerous when the sap was rising in the wood - towards the springtime. My father knew and remembered three or four people in the neighbourhood who had died of thorn poisoning. The invention of antibiotics has saved countless lives from that occupational hazard, not to mention the millions of lives saved from other diseases such as TB which was rampant at about the beginning of the 20th century.

To break the monotony of the long winter evenings, people used to visit each other far more than they do now. There were no telephones – families would simply turn up to spend the evening, after walking through the darkness with a storm lamp, or sometimes a Tilley lamp – which would be extinguished as soon as they arrived, so as not to waste paraffin. The evening would be spent chatting and catching up with the latest news or whatever had happened in the locality. The children were often encouraged to go to another room to play games – cards, snakes and ladders, ludo and draughts were very common in those days. By about midnight, the children would be falling asleep, and the adults would say 'We'd better make a move', and start to light the lamp. The Tilley would take up to ten minutes to light, until it was pumped up and started to hiss.

It was not only the visitors who were going out into the cold night air, but the hosts as well. They would put on their coats and boots so that they could escort their visitors to about half way home, and it was there that they said their goodbyes.

It seems to me that the motor car and the TV have put an end to that way of life for ever. In those days, there seemed to be more time for everything, but more importantly, to think about everyone else.

One very old practice that has died out with the introduction of the telephone is the putting out of 'a mark' as it was called. If there was an emergency on one of the farms, say an illness, or one of the animals was in trouble or difficulty, the farmer or his wife would take a couple of white flour sacks and hang them out somewhere visible from the surrounding farms – say on a tree, bush or gate. As soon as the 'marks' were spotted, everyone put down their tools and ran to see what was wrong, and how they could help. This practice had survived from the time of stone-age man, when beacons would be lit on hill tops as a warning of possible attacks by other tribes. There are other examples of such signals – e.g. the Native American Indian lighting a fire and sending smoke signals to warn others, or invite them for a meeting. With the disappearance of the old customs and traditions, practices that have lasted from thousands of years have disappeared within my lifetime.

CHAPTER 15

Places of Worship

The first difference that someone returning to his/her native parish nowadays would notice (whether in North or South Wales) is the number of chapels that have been closed. Some have been left to decay, others have been converted into houses. Seeing a well-built chapel with beautiful solid architecture being left to rot is a sad sight: the window panes cracking, the slates slipping, and the guttering hanging off by one screw. Most of these places were built less than two hundred years ago, to cater for the spiritual needs of the local people.

Not only was a chapel built, but also a Manse for the minister, as well as a house for the caretaker who looked after the chapel and cleaned it. In some places, there was also a vestry built for prayer meetings as well as for making tea or refreshments during funerals or singing festivals – the latter used to be held several times a year.

Over a hundred years ago, in some chapels, the biggest meeting of the year, the '*cwrdd mawr*', would start at seven thirty in the morning. There would be three guest preachers, preaching and praying alternately, with only a hymn sang between each sermon until dinner time, when everyone would eat in the vestry. In the afternoon, the same procedure would be followed with three different preachers. It was a day devoted entirely to religion, with the secondary attraction of meeting and talking to old friends. As in medieval times, a whole day was devoted to this.

When I was younger, all the churches and chapels used to put one day of the year aside for the harvest thanksgiving. In the churches, the day started with Holy Communion at ten thirty, followed at two o'clock by the Litany and a sermon, and at six thirty there was evensong and a sermon, given by the invited guest preacher. This practice has been abandoned, and there is no longer a day set aside for the Thanksgiving in the churches. There are only two services set aside for this purpose on a Sunday. By not setting aside a working day, we have lost something that was traditional, and not only to do with religion. Religion, in my opinion, imparted a sense of unity (everyone sharing a common belief), and by abandoning

✗ true of the 3 churches in Llangeler old parish but midweek as in the old days in Penboyr - ie St.Llawddog and St Barnabas.

149

these religious practices, we lose not just religion but that sense of unity.

It used to be that there was only one Holy Communion a month in each church, apart from Christmas and Harvest Thanksgiving. In a Communion service there was never a sermon. The clergyman would read some words of St Paul from the Common Prayer, and that was sufficient. The ten commandments were read in full. The Church has now done away with the Common Prayer Book which was in use from the sixteenth century, and in so doing, has taken away something fundamental and dear to all who used it. The beauty and musicality of the language was something deep and lived within our souls.

During the depression of the 1920's and 1930's, the churches and chapels were well attended, and again the same occurred during the war years. It was as though, during hard times, people felt the need to congregate together - safety in numbers – and a need to appeal to and trust in a higher power. With the coming of the affluent society, things have changed. For instance, the shops used to close on a Saturday, and remained closed until the following Monday morning. No-one had to work on a Sunday, apart from

✗ Nowadays the Book of 150 Common Prayer used in the Church in Wales is a revised edition.

people working in the essential services – such as nurses and doctors in hospitals, emergency services, and creameries. It now feels as though the days of the master and servant have returned, and that we live in an age of spending and greed.

Another change which the churches and chapels have had to face is the scarcity of ordained ministers of religion. Nowadays, a vicar or minister is responsible for several churches or chapels, and it is impossible for him/her to hold two services in each place of worship. In my own parish, of the three churches which used to have a vicar and a curate, there is now only one vicar in charge of two parishes with five churches.

I came across some old churchwarden's accounts sent in by someone to *The Countryman* (Kirby, 1957, p.791). The following are some of the accounts for the year 1807 – 08:

		s.d
Oct 2	*Relieved a traveller*	*1.0*
Oct 3	*Sparrows*	*4*
Oct 5	*1 hedgehog*	*4*
	2 Ditto	*8*
Nov 1	*3 hedgehogs*	*1.0*

Nov 5	Paid the Ringers	2.6
Nov 12	Relieved a Vagrant	6
Nov 29	Sparrows	4
Dec 1	2 Hedge Hogs	8
Dec 4	Paid... for the Bell, carriage and Expenses	15.0
Dec 29	Sparrows	2
Dec 30	A man and Mortar to Church	1.6
Jan 1	Wm Wrighton a Fox	1.0
Jan 9	for a Poll catt	1.0
Jan 20	Sparrows	4½
Jan 29	Paid for a fox	1.0
Feb 6	Paid at Mr Allcocks on the Bell Account	14.0

The payments for the destruction of vermin are curiously unecclesiastical but the charges were fixed by the vestry.... After an organ was installed in 1860, the organist got paid 50s a year, later raised to 70s. The blower supplied the wind for 5s a year.

Looking back, there has been a church in nearly every parish since about the sixth century AD, all of whom have had to change with the times, but it seems to me that the rate of change now is out of control, and increasing exponentially. There are too many sounds of the countryside, familiar to me in my time, which have gone forever, never to be heard again. I hope that the sound of church bells will not fall silent, as has the swish and groan of the water wheel on the farms and woollen mills, the laughter of young people in the fields, the whistle and puffing of the steam locomotive, or the rumble of a steel band of a cartwheel on the cobbles.

CHAPTER 16
Travel and Transport

There don't seem to be any records or descriptions of the journeys people made on foot, say, over a hundred years ago. The probable explanation is that people in general were unable to read or write. In any case, the only descriptions I have received have been verbal accounts given by my parents and older relatives, who recounted the stories told to them by their forefathers. One example is how people walked from every corner of Wales to Llangeitho in North Cardiganshire to hear Daniel Rowlands preach. They started in small numbers, and grew into larger crowds as they arrived nearer their destination in Cardiganshire, but no details have been recorded. I also remember my Uncle recounting the story of Siôn Owain, the old miller from North Wales, who walked all the way to Glastonbury to see the Tree of Joseph in bloom, and to return with a sprig to keep away evil spirits. He accomplished this journey although he only knew two words of English – 'stick' and 'Joseph'. If only he had kept a diary, telling us where he had stayed the nights. As I've mentioned before The Tree of Joseph is sometimes called the Glastonbury Thorn. It flowers twice a year, and as I have said, there is a legend that Joseph of Aramathea came to Glastonbury where he stuck his stick into the ground and it subsequently grew.

During the seventeenth and at the beginning of the eighteenth century, young men from West Wales, particularly Cardiganshire, would make the long journey to the corn fields of Herefordshire, Gloucestershire, and Somerset to cut the corn. They travelled with their scythes on their backs, and slept in barns and haylofts en route, to save all the money they had earned to take home with them. As soon as the South Wales coalfields opened, the tradition of the reaper making the annual harvest trip disappeared.

Men and women in the 'old' days thought nothing of walking to London from West Wales. Women went to work in the gardens of the rich, and men would find work in Smithfield or Covent Garden. The drovers also travelled from West Wales with large herds of cattle and sheep to Smithfield in London. Geese and turkeys also walked to London from all over Britain.

I would imagine that women travelled in pairs or small groups for safety and many travellers sought accommodation. I quote from Everyone's Encyclopaedia, vol. 6, 1978, p.567:

> *The traveller has sought shelter on his journey at Inns from time immemorial. As travel facilities have progressed from primitive to the luxurious, so have Inns. There are several Inns mentioned in the Bible, the best known being the one that had no room at the time of the birth of Jesus. Since the time of the Roman Empire, Inns have been found on all principal routes, the customary sign being an Ivy Bush.*

As well as Inns, the traveller could find hospitality at monasteries and hospices where the monks would have accommodation prepared, ready for weary travellers on their journey:

> *After the departure of the Romans from Britain the wayfarer would find hospitality at monasteries and other religious houses. In time, the monks who had been detailed to look after guests took over hospices specially built for the purpose; sometimes the lord of the manor would provide a similar house. Innkeepers tended to become*

important citizens, and they were given a charter, as innholders, in 1514. The names of old inns and their signs often recall this early association with church and nobility; Arms, Manor House, the Castle, the Mitre. The Fighting Cock Inn at St Albans is reputed to be the oldest in Britain, dating from the 9th century.........

The typical inn of the time consisted of a central courtyard surrounded by galleried buildings, with rooms for guests, stables for horses and coaches; a number of ostlers and other servants would be employed. A marked decline in the use of roads followed the introduction of railways in 1840-50. Within a few years the stage coach had disappeared, and many inns either went out of business or reverted to ale-houses.

The stage coach was the first form of public transport that became commonplace from the mid 16th century – mostly for travellers who could not afford to go on horseback. People were carried inside the stage coach, and in the late seventeen hundreds, a basket called 'the conveniency' was fitted on to the roof to carry passengers as well as luggage. The fee for travelling on the roof was half the price of that for travelling on the inside. In 1784, the mail coach system was introduced by John Palmer - to replace the post boys previously employed. At the same time, a lighter coach, known as the fast coach, was introduced, which cut the length of time for the journey significantly.

The coach posing for a photograph at Henllan bridge (near Rhydfach, where they used to change the horses)

(John Thomas collection, Llyfrgell Genedlaethol Cymru, The National Library of Wales)

Mules were often used for transporting goods as well to the
swelling population in industrial South Wales (such as cheese,
butter, fruit, fish, meat, and clothing from the local woollen mills):

During the second half of the eighteen hundreds, the Great
Western Railway, or GWR as it was called, came as far as
Carmarthen, amongst other places. From Carmarthen, it snaked its
way out in different directions. The line most familiar to me was
the one coming to Cynwyl Elfed. From there, it followed the river
Gwili to Llanpumsaint and Pencader. Between these two stations
the line ran through a tunnel, which is the longest in the County,
This tunnel lies under the summit of a range of hills which form a
watershed – the water flowing South from here towards
Carmarthen Bay, and North towards Cardigan Bay. Incidentally, it
was near this tunnel that the Royal train stopped for King George
VIth and Queen Elizabeth to stay the night - during the Royal tour
of Wales after the Coronation.

According to D. Morgan (1909, p. 82), Pencader was the junction
for the GWR branch line to Newcastle Emlyn, with stations at
Llandysul and Henllan. The line ended at Newcastle Emlyn, and
was run by the 'Manchester and Milford Railway' until 1906,

when it was taken over by GWR. Northwards from Pencader, the line to Aberystwyth went through the stations New Quay Road, Maesycrugiau, and Llanybydder, and entered Cardiganshire near Lampeter, following the River Teifi.

Milk churns being loaded on to a train to be transported to the city

(The Farmers' Weekly Collection, MERL, University of Reading)

In Carmarthenshire, the first passenger railway opened about 1840, but it was many years before it reached Llandysul and Newcastle Emlyn. Hundreds of men were employed working on the railways which included track laying, bridge building, and the construction of cuttings and tunnels. The railway companies therefore had to acquire many horses to pull all the carts and wagons.

I would like to include here an item of interest which I found in Thorley's Farmers' Almanack (1935, p. 30):

> *Duke, a bay shire horse, owned by the LMS Railway Company, has accomplished a magnificent feat by pulling a load of nearly eight tons out of the Maryport railway goods yard. A steel girder weighing 5 tons 12 cwt was placed on a timber weighing 2 tons. When it was found that there was not enough room to use chain horses, Duke was harnessed to the timber and made to pull the 7¾ tons himself. Once on the road, three other chain horses were harnessed in addition, and away they went for half a mile through the town. The unusual sight nowadays of four horses pulling in single file attracted as much attention as a circus procession. Duke is a shire horse, 17 hands high, powerfully built, and weighing nearly a ton.*

The advent of the railways meant that cattle could be transported very quickly to London from West Wales (that meant that there was no longer a need for the drovers who used to drive the cattle for long distances). Most of the cattle markets opened near the railway stations, where cattle could be loaded on to the railway trucks from the pens.

A typical scene of a cattle fair from the early eighteen hundreds
(The John Thomas collection, Llyfrgell Genedlaethol Cymru, The National Library of Wales))

Nowadays, big lorries have to be used on already overcrowded roads, because now we have lost the network of railways and small stations.

I suppose that when the first car was seen on the roads, no-one ever imagined that it would have any effect on how we lived – because, to most people, walking or horse riding was the normal form of transport in any locality. Longer distances required going by coach or train.

A common form of transport in those days was also by ox and cart. This method was followed by travelling by pack mules – these were used in some parts of Wales until the beginning of the twentieth century.

A carrier with his mules

During the next six or seven generations, the horse, cart, trap, gambo or waggon became the preferred form of transport, which used dusty untarred roads. But nowadays, the roads belong to the internal combustion engine, with its speed and noise. The road no longer belongs to the people whose land it passes through, and those people no longer bear responsibility for the road's upkeep. The leisurely pace and style of the horse and gambo have become aliens in their own home, as have the traditions of the people who used them.

Before I end this chapter, I will give a brief account what my father told me about his first trip to the market town of Carmarthen, about fourteen miles away. I heard similar accounts from two of my uncles, my father's brothers – so I can vouch for the veracity of the story. When they had reached the ages of twelve or thirteen, the boys were allowed to go with their father - my grandfather - to the market (in order to broaden their horizons, and to provide a small step towards independence).

After harnessing (or 'dressing' as it was called) one of the horses, it was put in the shafts of the gambo – the light two-wheeled vehicle, not as heavy as the tub cart. The gambo was then loaded with butter, cheese, vegetables and root crops, and they were off. The starting time was 3am:

> *In an unearthly silence, long before the first cockcrow*
> *disturbed the most nervous of ghosts, and under a violet*
> *canopy dotted with ruby lights that served to accentuate the*

blackness, the word of command would be given, and we were off. (D Parry Jones, 1948, p33)

The journey took about four hours, and as soon as they were on the main road (which in those days was not tarred as it is now) the going was quite easy, being mostly flat or downhill. Grandfather would point out different landmarks when it grew light enough to see. One landmark was a place on the moor where there was a notorious quarry. This quarry had been used as a hiding place for one of the highwaymen in days gone by – a place from which it was easy to disappear and escape across the moor into the mist.

As the party started descending towards Cwmduad, to the right was Clawddmawr, a big hedge, about 10ft high x 10ft wide, and very long. It has probably been there since the Stone Age, and has features in common with Watt's dyke in Wiltshire.

Then the road ran parallel with a stream called the Cloddi and after Cwmduad, the Cloddi joins the river Duad (which arises near a farm called Blaenduad). Then, the travellers passed through Cynwil, which was probably awakened very early every market day by the sound of the horseshoes and the rumble of the steel bands on the wheels of the carts. Half a mile further on, near Cynwil railway station, the river joined the river Gwili. From there, the road, river and railway ran parallel with each other. It was the custom in those days for a farmer to stop at a certain Inn to give the horse a break, and also for the people to stretch their legs. My grandfather's watering hole was the Rock and Fountain, about halfway through the journey, so that man and beast could have refreshment. In the winter months, the ice had to be broken in the trough for the horse, before going in for a cold pint.

> *The Inns until then had retained much of their traditional usefulness. They were on the wayside to serve the needs of the wayfarer there were no restrictions, they opened early and closed late. Looking back over the years upon this old-world scene, it presents itself to me in some of its aspects as a successor of a medieval pilgrimage making its way to a religious house of early fame.* (D Parry Jones, 1948, p.34)

(The mention of pilgrims reminds me of the pilgrims going to Canterbury, to the place where Thomas a Becket was murdered in 1170, and the fact that as a result, a new word was added to the

English language. The canter is the pace at which these pilgrims usually rode).

But I divert – back to the market day, and travellers. As they entered Carmarthen, dawn was losing itself into day. The young boys, aged about twelve to thirteen, must have marvelled at seeing the horses being unharnessed in the market yard and led out to the Rose and Crown – because that was where Grandfather had always stabled, and his father before him, and also my father as well, before he finished going to the market in a horse and cart for ever. At the Rose and Crown the horses entered through the same door as the people. Then the horses went out through the back door to the yard and stables to be looked after until it was time to go home.

During the monthly fairs that were held there, all kinds of livestock were sold: horses, cattle, sheep, pigs, and poultry.

The hustle and bustle of market day

(The John Thomas collection, Llyfrgell Genedlaethol Cymru, The National Library of Wales)

One fair in the autumn was famous for the numbers of geese. They were sold separately from the cattle – at the top end of Lammas Street near Goose Lane, which still retains the name. After the geese were sold, they were herded to the railway station to be taken away. Before the railways appeared, the geese were walked to London, being herded by gossards. The latter carried long sticks with red flags attached at one end, to stop the geese straying. It was a very common practice that, if there was a suitable river like the Thames flowing in the right direction, to allow the geese to swim for a good part of the journey.

In this day and age, it is difficult to imagine the pace at which people moved. It wasn't the throttle and gear lever but the animals that decided the pace of travel.

This is the last paragraph in this book. I hope the reader has enjoyed reading it as much as I have enjoyed writing it. In the name of progress, nothing much has survived of the farm machinery that I remember – the butter churn, the separator, cheese press, the water wheel, the barn threshing machine, the winnowing machine, and the chaff cutter, to name but a few. If you, as the reader feel there are some items of interest here, please pass them on to the younger generation to enjoy and, hopefully, to pass them on in turn.

BIBLIOGRAPHY

Parry Jones, D. (1948), *Welsh Country Upbringing*,
                Toronto BT Batsford Ltd., London, New York, Sydney

Thorley's Farmers' Almanack (1935), Joseph Thorley, Kings Cross, London

Parry Jones, D. (1953), *Welsh Legends,* BT Batsford Ltd, London

Jones, Daniel E. (1899), *Hanes Plwyfi Llangeler a Phenboyr* Gomerian Press

The Countryman (Winter 1956), ed. John Cripps, Burford, Oxfordshire

The Countryman (Winter 1957), ed. John Cripps, Burford, Oxfordshire

Parry Jones, D. (1964), *Welsh Children's Games and Pastimes*, Gee and Sons
                Ltd, Denbigh

Morgan, D. (1909), *The Story of Carmarthenshire,* The Educational
                Publishing Company Ltd.
                Trade Street, Cardiff

The Countryman, (Spring 1957), p.166 '*Texts in Stone*' ed. John Cripps,
                Burford, Oxfordshire

Everyman's Encyclopaedia (1978) ed. DA Girling, JMDent & Sons, Ltd.,
                London, Melbourne, Toronto